GOD
Only Knows

A Family's Story of Survival: Fueled by Faith,
Perseverance, and a Never-Ending Sense of Humor

KENNEDY OLIVER

ARCHWAY
PUBLISHING

This book is a work of non-fiction. Unless otherwise noted, the author and the publisher make no explicit guarantees as to the accuracy of the information contained in this book and in some cases, names of people and places have been altered to protect their privacy.

Scripture quotations are taken from the Holy Bible, New Living Translation, copyright ©1996, 2004, 2007, 2013, 2015 by Tyndale House Foundation. Used by permission of Tyndale House Publishers, Inc., Carol Stream, Illinois 60188. All rights reserved.

Archway Publishing books may be ordered through booksellers or by contacting:

Archway Publishing
1663 Liberty Drive
Bloomington, IN 47403
www.archwaypublishing.com
1 (888) 242-5904

Because of the dynamic nature of the Internet, any web addresses or links contained in this book may have changed since publication and may no longer be valid. The views expressed in this work are solely those of the author and do not necessarily reflect the views of the publisher, and the publisher hereby disclaims any responsibility for them.

Any people depicted in stock imagery provided by Thinkstock are models, and such images are being used for illustrative purposes only. Certain stock imagery © Thinkstock.

ISBN: 978-1-4808-5844-2 (sc)
ISBN: 978-1-4808-5843-5 (hc)
ISBN: 978-1-4808-5845-9 (e)

Library of Congress Control Number: 2018902248

Print information available on the last page.

Archway Publishing rev. date: 03/09/2018

Contents

Acknowledgments

I am so grateful for the encouragement I have received in getting this story out of my head and into print. The writing part happened quickly because I lived this experience. This made it easy to tell. However, the editing was an entirely different story. You see, I'm a math teacher, and writing is not something that I do very often. Writing a book was not on my bucket list and was not something that I would have ever dreamed of doing. Therefore, I would like to thank the editors, the encouragers, the doctors who stood by us, and the people who lived through this with me.

To Dr. Thomas Kennedy and Dr. Stephen Hopkinson: These are not your real names, of course, because for some reason writing a nonfiction book is nearly impossible if you are going to be totally truthful. However, you know who you are! To say thank you to both of you is nowhere near enough! You use your gifts every day to help others, and you stuck with us when nobody else would. We love you, and we are forever grateful!

To our families … Rae and Ben, our parents, our brothers and sisters, and all your people … I can't even begin to imagine what the four of us would have done without you … we love you!

And finally, to "my people" … Austin, Lucy, and Chloë: You survived this with me. We've gotten through some very low lows together and have experienced completely what it means to rely on Him for everything. I love you, I love you, and I love you … mwah!

For the people searching for hope when everything seems hopeless, for those searching for answers when there are none to be found—be still and know that He is in control. All glory goes to God! He gives us hope, peace, and the power to keep moving forward.

Chapter 1

June 29, 2011

As I was finishing my shower, I heard the phone ringing. Hurriedly, I rinsed, and then quickly grabbed a towel. I hate it when I drip everywhere. Who was it calling now? Lately our phone had been ringing off the hook ... which is funny to say since hardly anybody has a phone anymore that is on the wall. At any rate, maybe it's my sister Anne calling about the girls. Maybe it's someone calling to ask how Austin is doing. Maybe it's ... oh, whatever; I just needed to get to the phone before it stopped ringing!

"Hello?" I said.

"Kennedy, this is Sharon at the hospital. Austin has taken a turn for the worse, and you are going to have to get here as soon as possible."

"What do you mean? I just talked to him a half an hour ago, and he said he was going to get to try some apple juice, which he was excited about, after having had nothing for four days. A turn for the worse? What does that even mean? Can I talk to him?"

"Kennedy, listen to me," Sharon replied. "Austin has a temperature of 103.6, he is very sick, and he will need emergency surgery today. You need to get here as soon as you can because decisions have to be made."

I hung up the phone and fell straight down to the cold tile. I was dripping wet, bleeding all over the floor from my own open wounds, and absolutely stunned. A turn for the worse? What could have possibly happened in the last half hour? How could this be? Oh, dear God … no!

The next hour or so was kind of a blur. I didn't know what to do. What time was it? What day was it? I felt like I hadn't slept in years. Okay, it was eight thirty in the morning. If I didn't get out of here soon, Lucy and Chloë would be walking in the door from swim practice and I couldn't deal with talking to them right now about their daddy. A ten-year-old and an eight-year-old who have already, in their short lives, watched their mom get sick every day and lay around lifeless half of the time do not deserve this! What do I do? Who can I call? Do I go by myself? Is this even really happening?

Dear God, no! What the hell are you thinking? You can't do this to us right now. Please God, please! He has to be okay! We can't live without him! Please heal him! Please!

As I dialed the phone, it seemed to take forever before my sister answered. She said, "Hello," but it was as if I couldn't hear a thing. Was this really my life?

After six long years of my own nightmarish health issues, now it was Austin's turn? From deep within my heart I was screaming, *He's so healthy! He takes care of us! How can this be happening? What are you even thinking, God? If this is Your plan, then it completely blows! You have a very horrible, really sucky, no-good plan! Whoever said Your plan was perfect? Liars! All of them! I hate them, and I hate You!*

"Hello! Anybody there? Kennedy?"

Oh goodness, I'd forgotten I was on the phone.

"Hello, Anne?"

"Ken, what's going on?"

"It's not good. He's not doing very good at all. They called and said that I have to get there as soon as possible. What if he dies? He can't die. I can't lose him! Holy crap, what is going on? How can this be happening? Our life is so f'd up!"

"Ken, listen to me! Romans 8:28! 'And we know that in all things God works for the good of those who love Him, who have been called according to His purpose.' You have to stay strong! It's your turn to take care of things. You can do this, Ken! The girls need you to stay strong!"

"But I'm sick too. I'm still bleeding! I've got blood running down my legs right now! Do you hear me? This can't be happening! I don't even know what to do! I have to go. I need to get to Austin. You have to get the girls and don't tell them anything. I will call you as soon as I know what's going on!"

"You cannot go alone. Someone should drive you. I will call someone to pick you up."

"I don't have time. I have to go. Please hug my girlies and tell them that Mommy and Daddy love them; and Anne, you have to pray like you've never prayed before!"

The first thing I did after leaving my house was call the hospital. I asked for Austin's nurse, Sharon. It felt like a month of Sundays before she answered the phone. In fact, as I waited, I couldn't help but think, *A month of Sundays? Where did that even come from?* In my opinion, a month of Mondays would be so much worse, and at that moment, while waiting for Austin's nurse to get on the phone, I felt like I'd been waiting for at least two months of Mondays!

"Hello, Kennedy. Are you on your way?" Sharon asked.

"Yes, I am. How is he doing, and what do you mean when you say he's taken a turn for the worse? I'm really freaking out here!"

"Oh honey, you need to stay calm. It just means that Austin

is not handling any liquid that we give him. His perforation has not closed. His fever has spiked so high because his infection is getting worse. He needs to have surgery today. We need to decide whether we do surgery here or whether we send him by ambulance to a bigger hospital. Try not to worry, honey."

"Have we even told you what we've been through over the last six years? Our life is nuts, and this is crazy that this is even happening, Sharon! We can't seem to catch a break, and we can't lose him! The girls and I need him!"

I broke into the ugly cry, and we got cut off because I was traveling into a valley. I knew what I had to do: pray. I had to pray.

"Oh, dear God, what the hell are you thinking? Please don't take him, God. We need him. His girls need him! Stop the infection now! You can do that, God! Heal him! I know You can! Please? Romans 8:28 … 'And we know that in all things God works for the good of those who love Him.' I love You, God, but I'm not happy with You right now. I don't get it. I'm trying to trust in Your plan, but I have to be honest, it's a really sucky, absolutely rotten, no good, very bad plan! God? Are you there? I can't survive without him. We can't survive without him! Can You save him, please?"

God only knows …

Chapter 2

Labor Day Weekend, 2005

Could we really sleep here? Was this really ours? We hadn't quite moved in, but we had our clothes and our mattresses were on the floor. The only bed fully set up was Chloë's and that was because she was two and still in a crib … not that she actually slept like a normal two-year-old, but that was life with Chloë. She seemed to have inherited her dad's sleep habits. They both have a lot of energy and don't need a lot of sleep. We had not yet received the home inspector's okay, but we were having a sleepover in our newly built, not quite finished, but absolutely beautiful home! I felt like we were breaking the law and we probably were, and the excitement was making my heart race. We had no window coverings and a lot of windows, so I felt like I was trying to hide inside a fish bowl where the world could see that we were not following the occupancy rules. It was exciting and nerve-wracking all at the same time. Austin was lying next to me and was out like a light. He was totally exhausted because he'd been working like a dog since April.

Actually, if you really knew Austin, you would know that he always works like that. He never stops moving until he lays his head on the pillow at night, and luckily for him he falls asleep instantly. I, on the other hand, need all the stars to align, the barometric pressure to be within 2 percent of perfect, and the temperature to be beyond ideal and then, just maybe, I will be able to fall asleep before midnight. I'm not blessed with the gift of sleep ease. Is that even a thing? Well, I don't care. I'm guessing you know what I mean and that some of you can relate.

My life, however, was perfect, and by that I mean I had three healthy girls and an amazing husband. I had a wonderful job as a high school math teacher, and we lived in a wonderful small town where we planned to raise our children. We'd just moved into our beautiful new home that we'd designed and general contracted ourselves. Austin had done a lot of the work, and I'd just added my two cents where necessary.

Our oldest daughter is Rae. She was presently starting her life as a college freshman. She'd just moved into a dorm room and was getting ready to start classes. She had her whole life in front of her and was very hard-working and determined. We had no doubt that she would do well. Our middle daughter, Lucy, was four years old and getting ready for her second year of preschool. She is our sweet girl with a take-life-as-it-comes attitude. Some would say she has an old soul. I would say she has a heart of gold, an inquisitive mind, and a faith that is already stronger than her Mommy's.

She said to me as we were setting up her room, "Mom, I think we should stop for a second. Let's thank God for all of it ... for my new room, for my teachers and my school, and for having Chloë sleep good in our new house. Let's tell Him to bring the "spector" tomorrow ... okay, Mom? Oh, and Mom? How about we also ask Him if we could get a puppy. I think a puppy would even help Chloë sleep better! Don't you think it's a great idea, Mom?"

Lucy is as smart as a whip and had heard everything we'd said. She knew we weren't supposed to be staying in our house yet without the housing inspector's approval, and she also knew that she would really like to add to our family in the form of a puppy. She even thought to use the angle of her active, non-sleeping little sister. Who knew, maybe there would be a puppy in our future? Probably not, though, if Austin had anything to say about it!

Finally, last but certainly not least, our youngest daughter is Chloë. She was two and full of life and she hadn't slept through the night yet. She's a daddy's girl. She and Austin had already spent many hours together being the night owls that they are. Chloë knows what she wants and what she doesn't, and there was no forcing that girl to do anything she didn't want to do! She was the only kid I knew that refused to take a bottle, refused to eat any kind of baby food whatsoever, and also refused to sleep if she wasn't in the mood. That was our Chloë, and we loved her like we loved all three of our girls!

Just hearing the unfamiliar sounds of the new house and thinking about all that we had to do to get settled before Austin and I got back to teaching on Tuesday was causing sleep to escape me. As I began to make lists in my head of all that needed to get done, that all-too-familiar voice rang out from above.

"Mom! Dad! Mom! Dad! Hey! It's Chloë! I here! Mom! Dad! I here! I up!"

I jumped off the mattress on the floor and made the first of many treks up the stairs, past Lucy's room and on to Chloë's room. This was the first of many times when I questioned why we thought it was a good idea to put the master bedroom on a different floor from the girls' rooms.

As I raced into Chloë's room, I said, "Hi, honey! What's the matter?"

"Hi, Mom! I up!" she replied in her low little voice.

"Chloë, honey, it's not time. It's the middle of the night, and you need to go back to sleep."

Chloë's response was most often, "No, I up, Mom!" and she

certainly did not disappoint me on the first night in our new house.

She and I spent the next hour together lying on the floor in her room.

I would tell her a story and try to get her back into sleep mode, and she would grab my face, and with her big brown eyes staring into mine, she would say, "I up, Mom. I up! Sing, Mom, k?"

She was so stinking cute! On many nights I would sing to her a made-up tune that listed everybody in our entire family of many aunts and uncles, cousins, grandparents, and beyond. I think on this first night it only took going through the tune fifty times before I could see the strong-willed two-year-old's eyes start to fade. I had done it on our very first night! I managed to get that Chloë-girl, as we like to call her, back to sleep without waking up her very tired daddy and then managed to get myself back into bed all before 2:00 a.m. I felt accomplished, at peace, and very proud of myself. With my heart full of gratitude, I drifted off to sleep.

I remember I prayed that night, "God, why am I so blessed? Only You know, and I just want to tell You, I'm so grateful!"

Austin and I had been married for six years. We were absolute soul mates! Before finding Austin, I didn't really think that was a real thing. One person in the entire world who completed me? I didn't believe it was possible. Well, it is a thing, and he most certainly does. That's not to say that we didn't have our struggles. We did, like everybody who is in a committed relationship, but at the end of the day, I wanted him beside me, and I wanted to walk through this life with him. They say if your marriage can survive building a house together, then you can make it through just about anything. I don't know who "they" really are or if that's even something "they" say, but I do know that we did survive it, and Austin was still my person and I was his. Could we truly stay strong through anything that came our way?

God only knows …

Chapter 3

January 2006

Oh wow, Christmas break flew by! I was not ready to go back to school yet. I felt completely exhausted ... pretty much all the time. I blamed Chloë, the non-sleeper. I thought that one-year-olds could sleep through the night. So, why couldn't our almost-three-year-old? We hadn't taken her out of her crib yet, but I think we were just afraid to. Austin wanted to get her a big bed for her birthday that month, but then what would we do? Believe it or not, this kid stayed put when she was in her crib. She had not attempted to climb out once! As I envisioned her in a big-girl bed, I knew that in no time at all she would be coming downstairs and climbing into bed with us every night. Don't get me wrong, I loved snuggling with my girlies in my bed, but this Chloë-girl, I'm afraid, would become a permanent fixture once she was able to hop out of bed at will. Oh goodness, what was I worried about? Austin was right; we couldn't have her in a crib forever.

Anyway, back to my crazy exhaustion. I didn't think it was all Chloë's fault. It probably didn't help that recently, every time I got my period, I felt like I was going to bleed to death. My mom just said, "Welcome to my world." Two of my three sisters also had similar experiences, but I could hardly stand it.

I felt like I needed to go to the doctor to see if it was normal or not. Goodness, I was only thirty-eight, and I felt like over the last several months my periods had lasted longer and the breaks in between had gotten shorter and shorter. Actually, I thought that I would add this to the list of questions I'm going to ask God when I meet him.

This is how I envisioned the conversation going:

"Hi, God!"

"Oh, hi, Kennedy! Welcome to heaven! I hope you enjoyed your life on earth. Do you have any questions for Me?"

I was sure He would ask me that because He already knew that I had a lot of questions.

"Well, God, it's funny You should ask, because I do have a couple."

"Okay, fire away. I'm all ears!"

This part kind of cracks me up because I bet He is ... all ears, I mean. Can you imagine all the stuff He has been listening to for all of time? I mean, I'm just one person, and I know I sure have prayed a boatload of crazy prayers over the years. Then multiply me times however many living creatures there are. Now that's a lot of things to listen to! Anyway, back to my conversation when I meet Him for the first time.

"Okay, God, here goes. About the male/female thing. I don't get why you made us so very completely different. I mean, what do men really have to deal with? They do have PMS, I'm sure of it, but they don't have to deal with menstruating ever! Why is that? I know, they couldn't handle it, but really? Oh, and another thing, when women are done having kids, don't you think it would have been a good idea to let their periods end? Actually, in my humble opinion, I don't think the whole menstruation thing needs to even happen until a woman is ready to have a baby. I think there should be some kind of switch or something, or maybe You could have made us so that a year before we wanted to have a baby we could take the let's-have-a-period-now pill and then deal with it only up until we were done having kids. Oh, and for now, I just have one more thing. The big O … can I ask about that, God? What were you thinking? For a man … simple, but for a woman? Kind of like me with sleep … all stars, planets, and every form of space junk needs to be in a specific spot, and then maybe, just maybe, it might happen. Really, God? Any answers?"

I envision Him stunned and then agreeing with me that maybe, just maybe, He didn't quite think it all the way through.

As far as getting an appointment with the doctor to get some stuff checked out, I guessed I would start with my gynecologist. It wasn't just the periods and the exhaustion. I had been having crazy headaches and chest pain too. What was that about? There was a specific ache way inside my left breast. It never really went away. I just didn't feel good. Pretty much just blah … everyone knows what blah means, right?

Blah would be like the moment before you throw up when you are thinking, *Am I going to get sick? Is there a reason for the excess spit in my mouth or is this in my head? Can I just swallow enough times, close my eyes, and wish it away, or should I be racing to the bathroom?* I think you get the picture.

My plan was to start with my GYN and then see where that went. At my appointment, the doctor had a few questions, "Kennedy, have you been stressed lately? Are you depressed? Your EKG was normal, and your blood work all came back normal too. I think we first should put you on the pill to regulate your periods, and if that doesn't work, we can investigate other options. You are done having children, right? Because if you are, we can talk about other measures to deal with your heavy cycle."

I thought to myself that maybe she was absolutely right. Everything was related. The chest pain, the headaches, the overall blah feeling, and the exhaustion were all due to the fact that my cycles were totally whacked, which I'm pretty sure is a medical term, isn't it? I just needed to try something to get my body regulated. It made sense, and yes, I thought that maybe I was depressed. Who wouldn't be depressed when they were bleeding more often than not?

Going on the pill and waiting for it all to improve sounded good to me and to Austin. I was positive he would appreciate it if I wasn't Miss Crabby Pants most of every month! It would also probably help all our moods if spring would just come soon. We'd dealt with a lot of sinus and ear infections with the girls and a winter of just not feeling all that great. I felt like we all needed something to help lift our spirits. Lucy and Chloë were practically on a daily, sometimes hourly, basis asking if we could get a puppy. Rae had even said she would love it if we got a dog. Austin, though, continued to say, "Absolutely not!" Not under any circumstances would he ever agree to getting a dog. Could we get him to give in?

God only knows …

Chapter 4

May 2006: Cooper Comes Home

"Mom, do you think we will ever get a puppy? Leah and Wesley got one. Lee got one, and Toby and Taffy have been with Anne for a real forever already. Are you thinking about it? Does saying you're thinking about it mean yes, Mom? Does thinking about it mean you maybe will say we will have one by summer? Mom, can you tell me what thinking for lots of seconds means? Mom, do you hear me? Mom? Are your ears hearing me, Mom?" That sweet Lucy was so persistent and so doggone cute! Sorry... I couldn't resist.

Chloë's contribution to the conversation went something like, "Yeah, they did. Yeah, Leah and Wes, Lee, and Anne, Mom? You thinking, Mom? Can you just say yes to the puppy, Mom? Thinking, Mom? Do you hear me? Mom, Mom, Mom!"

Chloë always thought that saying mom three times in a row and increasing her volume each time was the ticket. She actually was right because my response was usually, "Chloë! What? Yes, I hear you!" I would then look at her cute little fat face and agree to whatever.

Lucy would then have that sweet smile of triumph and then put her arm around Chloë as if to say, "Good job Chlō! We are a great pair!" They truly were/are ... you know what I mean.

It was their dad they should be working on. Not me. He was the one who needed the convincing. If I was a betting person, I would still place a bet against it ever happening, but that didn't stop me from doing a little research on the side. I knew if it was going to happen, the puppy would have to be non-shedding, not real big, not real small, not real difficult, and not much of a barker. I'm not sure if that's how a first puppy is ordered, but that was my goal.

Little did we know at the time, but our newest family member had already been born. I can't even recall how it happened or how I got Austin to agree. The weird thing was that neither of us had ever in our lives had a dog. We both grew up in animal-free homes. We were not pet people … or so I thought.

I remember the first day that we brought him home. Austin and I had traveled two hours north to get him from a place that only bred cockapoos, a mix between a cocker spaniel and a poodle. There was nothing quite like surprising a three- and five-year-old with a brand-new adorable puppy. We named him Cooper, and we fell in love with him immediately!

One of the cutest times with Cooper was when I looked out the window as Austin was mowing the lawn, and he was following right behind him. He became Austin's shadow. One time Austin had him outside while he was doing yard work, and he thought Cooper was right by his side. Austin was standing on the lawn below our front porch. The porch was about fifteen feet above him. Suddenly, Austin realized that Cooper wasn't there, so he started to call for him. He looked everywhere until he heard a squeaking sound above him. Cooper was up on the porch. There was a railing, of course, but Cooper was still pretty little.

Austin immediately said, "Cooper, stay! Stay, Cooper! Do not come through that rail. Cooper!"

The cutest dog ever fit right under the bottom of the porch

rail. Are you kidding me? Austin could see that this was not going to be good. The next thing he knew, Cooper was airborne! Thankfully, Mr. Big Hands, Austin Oliver, was ready! He said as he looked up, all he could see were boy puppy parts coming at him fast!

He said a quick prayer, "Please, God, let me catch this guy who is now a very important part of our family!"

God answered that prayer ... hallelujah! His name was now Super-Cooper! Who knew that cockapoos could fly?

As Cooper grew, we soon realized that he was a dog that we could easily train. He potty-trained pretty quickly, he learned how to fetch almost right away, and Austin even taught him to sit, roll over, and give a high ten. That's right, two paws up meeting the hands of anyone who asked. Wouldn't that actually be a high twenty? Anyway, Cooper was almost perfect. The only real issue we had with him lasted for the next several years: if he got outside without being on a leash, it was a huge struggle to get him to come back in our house. It was really crazy! So crazy that as the years went by, everyone in our neighborhood knew that if Cooper got out without a leash, we needed help! Every child and adult available would come running to help us. Sometimes treats worked, but Cooper was smart. He quickly learned that a hotdog, piece of dog biscuit, or anything for that matter, was something of which to be leery. He also mastered grabbing the treat and still escaping.

Another thing we noticed was how Cooper acted in our house. He was totally chill. He never chewed up things, and he rarely barked. He didn't stand at the door waiting to get out either. He pretty much did everything we asked him to do and was the best snuggler ever! Could we handle this dog we couldn't catch?

God only knows ...

Chapter 5

Fall 2007

On one occasion when Cooper escaped, I was trying to get to a meeting to discuss my upcoming surgery. I had tried everything to avoid this surgery, but nothing worked. My periods were out of control! I sometimes couldn't get through a class hour at school without having to excuse myself to run to the restroom. I felt like garbage almost all the time. A hysterectomy seemed like it was going to be the answer. I really didn't know how it worked if you had to have surgery in the middle of a school year, but I was reassured by my coworkers that it would all work out. The school district would get a substitute teacher for the time that I would be out, and that sub would hopefully be able to teach math.

This was pretty much how it went. The surgery was scheduled for November 21, 2007. I was going to be out of school for six weeks, and the plan was for me to get back to work after the Christmas break. The unfortunate part was having surgery the day before Thanksgiving, but this would allow me to miss the least amount of school because the students would be off for the holiday too. I felt bad for Lucy and Chloë because I was kind of ruining the holiday, but I knew that this six-week period in their lives would come and go and they probably wouldn't even remember it in the future. Lucy was in first grade and Chloë was not in school yet. I was looking forward to spending more time with her while I was home recovering between Thanksgiving and New Year's, as I knew that her school years were fast approaching.

The plan was to get ready to be gone from school for six weeks, prepare for surgery that would vastly improve my life, and hopefully enjoy the upcoming holiday season. Many women told me that I would feel so much better after this was done. It was surprising to me just how many women I knew who had already gone through a hysterectomy. They all had words of encouragement and told me that it would all go smoothly and I would be so happy afterward.

I joined a support group online called HysterSisters. This was a site where you could connect with women who had gone through similar health situations and maybe find out what to expect. Initially, it was great because it calmed me to know how many women had gone through what I was going through and had done just fine after having a hysterectomy. However, I needed to stop reading it after a while because it was also a site where you could read about all the things that could and did go wrong. Thankfully, I was confident that everything was going to be okay, and I had a sense of peace that we were doing the right thing. Austin and I both knew that we couldn't continue to live like we were living, and we were so looking forward to an end to the bleeding.

The night before surgery, I felt prepared and good about it. We sat down with Lucy and Chloë and explained what was going to happen. We told them that I would only be in the hospital for one or two nights and that I would soon feel much better! I remember making them a chocolate sheet cake because it was their favorite and it would be something special for them to have while I was in the hospital.

The pre-op plan was for me to have my uterus and cervix removed, but the surgeon would leave my ovaries. This would allow me to not have to deal with the instant effects of not having ovaries. My understanding was that with ovary removal you would go right into menopause, which was not a fun process. I was happy that we were going to be able to put that off until it happened naturally.

The morning of the surgery I met with my GYN, Dr. Adams, in the pre-op area, and we discussed the plan one last time. I remember being very calm and at peace with all of it.

The next thing I remember, as I was being wheeled down the hall to the operating room, was Dr. Adams coming to the side of the bed and saying something like, "Hey, Kennedy, I think we are going to do a laparoscopic supracervical hysterectomy."

My response was, "Huh? What's that and why? How is it different from what we were going to do?"

Her response was, "It will be better for you in the long run and a quicker, much easier recovery."

As you can imagine, while I was lying on the bed in the hallway on the way to the OR, not having Austin by my side, this caught me totally off guard. I don't remember what I said or if I even questioned her further. I do remember putting my trust in God that this was going to be okay even though I was superconfused and felt very out of control. Anybody who knows me knows that not being in control is very hard for me. I like to know the plan, double and triple check it, foresee any obstacles, and anticipate anything that might not go correctly so that I can be prepared. I knew this was not always possible in life, but I did my best to come close. This is also not how someone who puts their trust in God lives. Hey, I've never said that I've mastered the art of faith. I am definitely a work in progress! At any rate, this was what occurred the minute before entering the operating room for my hysterectomy, and it was very un-settling, to say the least.

Thankfully, according to my GYN, the surgery was text-book and all went according to plan ... her last minute plan, that is. Unfortunately, my experience with anesthesia was not so perfect. I woke up nauseous and throwing up, which was not much fun after surgery. This is one more thing I'm going mention to God when I meet Him face-to-face. I think it should be against the law for anyone who must go through surgery to also have to endure puking afterward. Oh, and another thing, sharing a hospital room with another patient who is throwing up should also be against the law. My roommate and I were dueling pukers. Now, that's not a melody that anyone should have to listen to. I remember my poor sweet little girls coming to visit their mommy on Thanksgiving Day, no less, in the hos-pital. They got their first exposure to my roommate's colorful language between hurls ... it was lovely—not!

I ended up staying in the hospital for two nights before be-ing discharged. Little did I know at the time, but this was only the beginning of a very long and very complicated journey. A journey where our faith would be tested, our marriage would be tested, and my physical strength would be tested further than I could have ever imagined. My control-freak personality would meet its match and be forced to the wayside while I would need to use every ounce of my soul to keep putting one foot in front of the other.

There were too many times over the next six years where I would have to specifically pray to God, "Please take over ... not that You haven't already, but what I'm saying is, please help me to let go. I know Your plan is perfect, and I know that I need to trust, but I also know that I'm really bad at it sometimes. If You could please help me do that better, I would be very grateful. Also, could You carry Lucy and Chloë through this because I am too weak to even hold them in my lap. This is breaking my heart and is something I'm going to complain to You about when I meet You face-to-face. Oh, and God, one more thing ... could we have that face-to-face meeting after my girls are all grown up? Oh, and just one more thing; I am in no way comparing my struggles to Your sacrifice. Sacrificing Your son was *huge* and something I cannot even imagine. Thanks a ton for that! Love You, God!"

Can I get through this?

God only knows ...

Chapter 6

December 2007–January 2008

What was going on? I felt like total garbage. I had no energy, and I'd started bleeding again. The surgery was supposed to be the solution that was going to end that. I could hardly get off the couch, and I felt so bad because the holidays were miserable! The day we went to cut down our Christmas tree was especially depressing. My niece, Jessica, went along with us to help and make it fun for Lucy and Chloë. They totally adored her, and she always made life fun!

We pulled into our parking space at the tree farm, and Austin looked at me and said, "Honey, it's okay if you just sit in the car. The girls understand that you don't feel good."

My stubborn response was something like, "There is no way I'm missing this. I can do it!"

We all got out of the van, and it was a picture-perfect day for cutting down the Christmas tree! There was a light snow falling, and the temperature was a wonderful thirty degrees, which is balmy for Wisconsin in December. Jessica got the girls out, and they were adorable in their snow gear and oh so excited!

I remember Lucy saying, "Come on, Mom! You can do it! We promise to not go far!"

Sure enough, we found our tree only about ten yards from

the van. I was pretty sure God had something to do with this plan. However, what happened next was not so pretty. I could feel the nausea getting to me. It was one of those occasions where I tried to keep swallowing and wishing it away, but my mouth started to water, and even though I was out in the winter weather, I broke into a cold, nasty sweat. So, yes, I spoiled our Rockefeller moment. I proceeded to throw up right behind somebody else's choice for a Christmas tree right when they were taking their family picture. Can anyone say embarrassing? Oh, and another thing, have I mentioned how much I hate throwing up? I despise it more than a bad cold that lasts for months! I always feel like I'm somehow going to choke to death. Why do I continue to feel so lousy?

This would be the Christmas where the girls decorated the tree all by themselves while I was on the couch watching. I can remember feeling so emotional about it but so inspired by my six- and four-year-olds.

They would ask with the placement of almost every single ornament, "Is it good, Mom? Do you like it? Are you okay, Mom? Look at this one, Mom! Remember this one, Mom? This is my favwit!"

When Austin brought out the ladder for them to climb to the top, I wasn't okay. Our house had twenty-foot ceilings in the great room where we put our tree, so we always tried to get a pretty tall one. Ladders were always required, but watching my little girls climb to the top to put their ornaments as high as they could contributed to my nausea.

Chloë said, "Look, Mom, I'm almost taller than …" She then got sidetracked because she could see the dust on top of our entryway cabinetry and said, "Oh, Mom, it's vaawy duwty up there; you rewy need to dust."

With that Lucy chimed in, "Chloë! Mom can't dust! She can hardly get off the couch!"

Ugh, my girls were getting used to our new routine, and keeping the house clean also contributed to my nausea! I'm not a clean freak by any means, but I would get stressed at the sight of dust and stuff that's not put away.

At any rate, as I approached my six-week post-op timeline, I became more and more panicked because I wasn't feeling any better. I was still bleeding, I was totally exhausted, and I had a lot of pelvic pain. Why was I bleeding? That's why I had the surgery, right? I remember going to the doctor, and she said I should maybe extend my leave to eight weeks because I was just one of those slow healers. She also didn't really believe that I was bleeding. I recall the actual pelvic exam.

She said something like, "Oh my, you *are* bleeding a lot!"

I'd been saying that for a while but was not taken seriously. The other very unfortunate and sad thing that happened prior to that appointment was that I got word that my long-term substitute teacher had passed away from a complication with his heart. It was horribly sad, and it complicated things for me emotionally.

It was very stressful dealing with the emotions of my sub dying and feeling upset over not feeling any better as the days passed. I was also starting to lose weight. Only about ten pounds so far, but why? Actually, ten pounds in that short of time was kind of a lot! So, given that I was bleeding a lot and still had a lot of pelvic pain, my doctor suspected that I possibly had a hematoma, which is a collection of blood outside the blood vessels usually in liquid form. This might explain the pain I was in and the amount of bleeding I was experiencing. She made an appointment for me to have a pelvic ultrasound the next day at another facility.

Austin took me to the appointment for the ultrasound. I remember it being very painful and very bloody. The technician suggested that I call my doctor right away and have a CT scan done. Huh? For what? None of it really made sense to me. Was something really wrong? Did I have a hematoma? Why on earth was I bleeding? This is a funny phrase, "Why on earth?" My mom would say it all the time. If not on earth, then where? We've never been anywhere but on earth. Anyway, I digress ...

After the ultrasound, the technician couldn't really say anything and just told me that I would be hearing from my doctor for the results. I left there feeling totally lost. I felt like nobody really had a clue and that I was getting a glimpse of a medical system that, at times, felt very disjointed. The communication did not seem to be very good, to say the least.

I remember getting to our car and bawling, "What was going on, God? Why am I bleeding? Why am I in so much pain? Why do I have no energy and feel like I've been hit by a truck?"

Before even leaving the parking ramp of the facility, my phone started ringing. I answered it, thinking it might be my doctor with results or at least a plan for what we were going to do next.

"Hello?"

"Kennedy? It's Mom. Where are you?"

"Oh, hi, Mom. I'm sitting in the parking ramp of the ultrasound place with Austin. I just had a very miserable stick-the-wand-up-where-the-sun-doesn't-shine ultrasound."

"Well, you're never going to guess who I just ran into at the clinic. I just talked to Dr. Adams."

She happened to be my mom's GYN too.

"I ran into her in the hallway while I was taking Dad down to have labs done. She told me that you don't have a hematoma and that you are probably just stressed because your sub died. She said the best thing for you, at this point, is to get back to work. You are just becoming depressed from lying around and worrying."

I was absolutely, without a doubt, shocked, and I really

didn't have the words to describe how this made me feel. I remember going into my "become a zombie and don't say anything you'll regret" mode.

"Okay, Mom, thanks."

"Well, it seems to make sense, Kennedy. Honey, you know maybe you are feeling depressed about not being back at school."

"Do you think bleeding is caused by stress, Mom?"

"Oh honey, I don't know, of course it's not, but Dr. Adams just really thinks that ..."

I don't even know what was said after that. Why was my doctor talking about me to my mom in the hallway of the clinic? Was that a thing that doctors did? Are you kidding me? Why was I bleeding? Stress? Stress causes bleeding? What the heck? Why did I feel like garbage? Getting back to work would solve this? Why was I losing weight? Are you kidding me? Was I losing my mind? What was going on, God?

After coming home, I went straight to our bed, laid down, and stared at the ceiling. I had no energy to even cry.

I remember that Austin kept saying, "I'm so sorry, honey. Let me call Dr. Adams. This is crazy! Let me talk to her. She should be calling you, right? Didn't they say she would call? Why would she talk to your mom? Please let me call her."

I said no. I didn't want to talk to her. I didn't even want to deal with this. She saw how much blood there was. I didn't understand any of it. Why would she talk to my mom about my health? That made no sense. Why was I in so much pain? Why was I bleeding? A lot of questions without any answers ... ugh.

Austin then left to go get Lucy and Chloë. This was a Friday afternoon. No one from the clinic called with the results of the ultrasound. We went through the weekend with me bleeding and feeling miserable. Everyone knows how horrible it feels to go into the weekend with a medical issue. It sometimes feels like the worst medical issues happen on Friday nights right after clinics close. Can anyone relate to this or is it just me?

On Monday morning I found the courage to call into the clinic. I left a message for Dr. Adams to call me because I was still bleeding and in pain. At around five o'clock that evening, the phone rang. The point is, I waited all day! Austin answered and said it was the doctor's nurse calling and handed me the phone. Of course it was her nurse. Why would she call herself? In my experience so far, you rarely get to talk to the actual doctor.

"Hi, Kennedy, this is Jenny, Dr. Adams's nurse. The results of the ultrasound show that you don't have a hematoma. Dr. Adams has been consulting with other doctors about you. She thinks that, unfortunately, you are one of those people who, even though you've had a hysterectomy, are going to continue to have a monthly bleed because we left your cervix. So, Dr. Adams wants you to monitor it over the next four to six months and let us know if you have any further questions. Oh, and Kennedy, she thinks you should probably try to get back to work." Long pause. "Kennedy? Are you there?"

"Yes … I thought that the whole point of having the hysterectomy was so that I would no longer bleed."

"Yes, but you opted for the supracervical hysterectomy, and there is a very small percentage of women who will continue to bleed. Unfortunately, you are in that percentage. So, good luck to you."

What just happened? Were they really just blowing me off? Since when had I opted for the supracervical? I was in the hallway going into surgery when I was informed it was happening! I didn't even know what to think! Where do I turn? Physically, could I teach? Are you kidding me? I'm bleeding! I am in total pain! What the hell was going on? I felt like I'd been hit by not just a truck, but a truck carrying other trucks and coming down a mountain at seventy miles per hour! How in the world was I supposed to deal with this?

God only knows …

Chapter 7

A Second Opinion

A ustin had taken Chloë to my sister Anne's house, gotten Lucy on the school bus, and was on his way to school. I was in the middle of a raging emotional panic attack because I was scheduled to go back to work in a week and a half. God knew I needed an intervention. That's when the phone rang.

I answered, "Hello?"

"Ken? Are you okay? It's Joy … Ken? What's wrong? Ken?"

I couldn't even catch my breath in between sobs.

"I don't know what to do. I don't know where to turn. I am sick. I am in pain. I'm bleeding, and I feel like I'm going to die."

"I think it's time to get a second opinion. This isn't right."

"I can't. She's been my doctor since I was seventeen. I trusted her! I don't even know what is going on? My body is so messed up!"

"People get second opinions all the time. You can, and you need to. You need to for the girls and for Austin. You need to for yourself!"

"I have no idea who to even call. I feel so lost."

"Let me take care of it. I will ask around today and get back to you."

My sister Joy worked at a hospital in the education

department where she led and scheduled all types of classes. She had connections with people because of this and had friends who had suggestions for a second opinion. The next thing I knew, I was on the phone with a nurse from a women's health clinic. She had me explain the whole story and determined that, although the GYN I was trying to see was very busy, she would absolutely work me into her schedule. The plan was for me to see the nurse practitioner at the clinic first because it would be easier to get an appointment with her. They would schedule the appointment on a day that the doctor was in the clinic too, so that maybe I could see her also. I felt like this was the first time in a long time that I was being listened to and actually *heard*.

The day of the appointment I was a nervous wreck. Austin was unable to get the day off to go with me, so I had my friend Kate take me, which was a great comfort. I met with the nurse practitioner first and went over the whole story. She listened to everything but didn't do an exam because she didn't want to put me through that without the doctor. She asked about the pathology report from the first surgery. I told her that they had told me everything was normal. She said they would get a copy of it. She also said that she had an idea of what was going on and was really glad that I'd come to them. She said she was so sorry for what I had been through and thought that they could for sure help me. She said she was going to check with the doctor to see if she had time to see me.

The next thing I knew, they were both walking back into the room. Dr. Brown and the nurse practitioner couldn't have been nicer and more understanding. They also had the pathology report from the first surgery, which stated that I had significant adenomyosis. This would explain my very heavy bleeding prior to surgery.

"Huh? Dr. Adams told me it was normal. How can that be? I am so confused. Is having significant adenomyosis normal?"

I was in shock, to say the least. She then did an exam. Now, pelvic exams are not fun, and for reasons that I'm not going to go into, they are not fun for me. Actually, who really enjoys them? I tend to break out into an allover body rash, shake, and tense up like a weight lifter does before attempting to lift the weight of his or her life. Despite the doctor's reassurances and attempts at helping me to feel calm, this exam was not any different. The first thing she realized right away was how much I was bleeding. It was "significant" in her words. She also commented on an area that had been torn in the past and did not heal well. She asked if intercourse was painful to which I replied, "Yes!" She also said that she was really glad that I'd had the courage to come in and get a second opinion. She acknowledged how it wasn't an easy thing to do. After the exam, she told me that I could get dressed and said that she would meet with me in another room to talk about what she thought.

Since Kate had given me a ride to the appointment, I invited her into the meeting with Dr. Brown because I thought two people hearing the plan was better for my stressed-out, overly tired, totally emotional brain. Dr. Brown explained that it appeared that the way the first surgery was done was causing me to continually bleed. I won't get into the details of what was wrong, but it made perfect sense. Her recommendation was to take me back to the OR and take the rest of my cervix, which would ensure that the bleeding would stop. She also suggested repairing the area that was causing me pain during intercourse. She said that she wouldn't want to live like I was living and could totally understand why I felt like total garbage.

I had a really hard time wrapping my head around the fact that one surgery was now turning into two, but I felt hopeful at the chance that I would get my life back.

I remember that while I was sitting there taking in all the information, the rash that had started from the pelvic exam now was creeping its way up to my neck. Guess what? My rash does not discriminate. It doesn't only appear for physical situations that are uncomfortable. It rears its lovely head at a thought, a nervous social situation, and yes, even when a doctor was explaining how I could be healed.

I left the office with a nervous sense of hope and a renewed faith in the medical world. I knew that I had to go through with the second surgery and that it was all going to be okay. It meant that I would have to take more time off from school, but it also meant that the sooner we scheduled it, the sooner I would be back to running around with my sweet girls. Was this the answer?

God only knows …

Chapter 8

Surgery #2

The night before surgery I was nervous, excited to finally start to feel better, and really kind of shocked that we were even having to talk to Lucy and Chloë about what to expect over the next couple of days. Remember, they were only five and six years old. We had just celebrated Chloë's birthday on January 24, and Lucy didn't turn seven until February 23. This was February 18, 2008, the eve of surgery number two and hopefully the end to this craziness.

As we were getting the girls ready to go sleep at Anne's house since we had to leave very early the next morning, Chloë, in her sweet little low voice said, "Mom, pwomise that this is the last soogewy, k?"

Lucy right away jumped in with, "Chloë, Mom can't promise! Only God knows what will happen … but, Mom? Do you really think this will make you all better and that it might be the last one?"

I tried to reassure the girls that we felt confident that this was going to fix things and that I would soon feel better.

Austin chimed in with, "We promise, girls, that Mom is going to come home from the hospital and get better with each passing day. We are so proud of you two, and we love you very much! Aunt Anne will bring you to the hospital to see Mom tomorrow night, okay? Now, who's going to help take the chocolate sheet cake that Mom made out to the car?"

I'd made a cake for the first surgery, so to help comfort them, we were sending them to Anne's house with another cake. Besides, it was Anne's favorite too!

The surgery went very well. They took my cervix, left fallopian tube, and my appendix. I'm not sure why they took that, but I guess we'll never have to worry about that rupturing. I spent another two nights in the hospital, but then came home. The recovery was not easy, but the care I received from the clinic was excellent. They called me every day to see how I was doing. One of the best things was that I finally wasn't bleeding. This was a great relief, and although I felt like I was in some very weird never-ending dream, I thought it would be coming to an end soon.

I went to my first post-op appointment and was down about twenty pounds from the beginning of the journey. I really had no appetite, but I continued to try to eat. I didn't really know why I was losing weight. However, I had been through a lot! Dr. Brown said that my body had been through so much and that I should think about not going back to school until the fall. Are you kidding me? I was only supposed to be out six weeks! Unfortunately, she was right. There was no way that I could teach in the shape I was in.

On top of just recovering from surgery, I was having other unfortunate symptoms. I had ongoing chest pain, frequent gallbladder attacks, and almost constant headaches. My entire system seemed to be totally whacked! Let me remind you, since writing this I've discovered that "whacked" is actually not a medical term; however, it is a term that adequately described my condition. I just felt like junk all the time! Nobody could figure out why. My labs always came back normal, and all tests turned up nothing. What was going on? I started to feel like maybe I was going crazy!

At about seven weeks post-op, I went back to Dr. Brown so that she could see how everything was healing. I told her that I still felt like garbage, and she said that it was understandable, given what I had been through. She told me that I needed to be patient and that it took a long time to recover from one major surgery, let alone two! Dr. Brown did an exam and said that everything looked like it was healing nicely. She still felt that I should take it easy, but said that the incision was healed enough inside that she gave me the okay for activity.

Given how I felt, I wasn't going to go out and start training for my next marathon or anything. And besides, that would imply that I liked to run, which I do not. I would rather pick rocks out of a twenty-acre field on a one-hundred-degree day than go for a run. Is that clear enough for you? My best run was when I was in seventh grade. I ran the mile in seven minutes and four seconds. That was fast for me, and I absolutely hated all 424 seconds of it. I would, however, like to start doing some normal mom things. I really would just like to feel up to playing with my kids. That would be heavenly! I would also like to reconnect with my husband. Not that we aren't tight, but having two GYN surgeries over the course of six months had put a damper on all our physical activity, if you know what I mean. Am I really all healed?

God only knows …

Chapter 9

My Insides Explode

April 12, 2008, was a day that Austin and I will never forget. How do I even attempt to explain something so personal yet so significant? There are some things in life that you only tell a select few people, but when you try to explain your story in the form of a book, you must tell the whole story … even when it means sharing intimate details.

My prayer prior to writing this is, "Oh my goodness, God, please give me the words and calm my fears. Take away the anxiety that thinking about this event brings, and give me the ability to just write. I'm okay that I have the allover body rash while writing, but my fear is that it will become permanent. That's how traumatic this is. This is so unbelievable that many physicians we've talked to have never heard of this happening to someone. You have to admit, God, this part of the story is as crazy as hell, and from what I've read, hell is damn crazy! Please, God, walk with me like You always do, and make the rash go away eventually."

You know how there are times in your life that are etched in your mind forever? Like the day you got your driver's license, where you were on September 11, or that moment when your first child was born. This is one of those events. Just allowing myself to think about it can take me right back there. You see, Austin and I had not been intimate for months. After two surgeries on my parts down under, you can imagine that intimacy was the last thing on my mind, but it was also not an option. On the Saturday night after my doctor appointment where we'd gotten the okay to have sex, we did—or I should say, we tried.

It was immediate. It was like something out of a horror movie, but Austin and I were in the movie. It was a feeling that I will attempt to describe, but I doubt that words can adequately do it justice. Think of my vaginal area like a sock. At the end of the sock, where your toes go, is the top of my vagina. We're talking way up inside! This area was sewn shut after surgery number two. There is a top seam that Dr. Brown had told us was all healed and looked great. Pushing on it at all would be totally fine. Well, with that very first push, when Austin and I connected, there was a significant explosion. I felt like my insides had violently blown open. It was like a balloon had burst inside of me. There was even a sound to it. It was a sound like when you put your lips together, holding your breath for as long as you can, and then you let the air out with as much force as humanly possible. That was my vaginal cuff ripping apart all in one blow. That was inside my body, and it was not pretty. The pain was indescribable … there are not words in the English language that even come close to doing it justice!

The look on Austin's face was one of horror!

I immediately started yelling, "Get out! Get out now!"

He did, while I writhed in pain.

I remember saying to him, "My insides just literally exploded, and I'm going to throw up! I'm pretty sure I might die! Please help me!"

He tried to help me get up, but I was in extreme pain. Upon standing, I doubled over in pain. I thought for sure I would faint. He carried me to the bathroom, where I got violently sick.

I didn't say it, but I thought, *This is when we should call 911.* The crazy thing was that I also thought, *There is no way that I am telling anyone, especially our small-town EMS people, what just happened!* This is where profanity takes over my thoughts. You can just imagine it. Yes, Christians use profanity. This Christian does, and this event warranted it! God knows this, and I'm pretty sure He agrees ... or at least I feel like He would.

There was also a lot of blood, and it was very scary! We had Dr. Brown's pager number, and she had said we could call at any time. We didn't hesitate even though it was late at night. She called back, and she first talked to Austin. He then put me on the phone, and I tried to explain what had happened. I told her that I was in extreme pain and was bleeding a lot.

She replied with, "I'm sure it's just scar tissue that you felt, and it's not really that serious. Nothing could have come apart because you are all healed. Take some pain medicine and call me in the morning if it doesn't improve."

Seriously? I just told you that my insides exploded, I'm in extreme pain, and I'm bleeding a lot. You want me to take a pill and call you in the morning? Are you kidding me? Believe it or not, that's what we did. The doctor knows best, right? I thought, *I must be a person who can't handle much. I must have a very low pain tolerance.* That is what I kept telling myself.

I took the pain meds, which make me nauseous, by the way, and I tried to find a comfortable position to sleep. This truly was one of the longest nights of my life. By morning, I could hardly walk across the room. Austin had to help me or I would have passed out. The pain was incredible, and the bleeding continued. We paged Dr. Brown again and told her we were going to the emergency room. She said she would meet us there ... thank goodness! She still tried to reassure me that it was probably just scar tissue.

I remember thinking, *You are probably right, but I really*

feel like I could die. I guess I can't handle the pain caused from something so simple like scar tissue. What can I say? I am a total wimp!

We made a call to our neighbors, Kate and Ted, to see if one of them could come down to be with the girls, who were still in bed. Ted came down right away, and we headed to the hospital.

I prayed all the way to the hospital, "Oh God, what is going on? Is this in my head, or did my insides really blow up? I can't handle this pain anymore. I mean, I can, but God? I really don't want to! Please help me … please, God! I'm kind of begging because this is so excruciating. Please be with Lucy and Chloë. Oh, my sweet little girls … seriously, God? If you could just get my sister to our house before they wake up. They like Ted, but I really just want Anne to be there to explain to them where we are. Why, God, do we have to try to explain this to them? I really don't want anybody to know about this. Did we do something wrong? What did we do, God? I feel like we are cursed or something. We aren't cursed, right? That's not even a thing, right? Help us, and please don't leave us! I'm scared, God."

Thankfully, Dr. Brown had called ahead to the hospital to explain that we were coming, so they were ready for us. We didn't have to wait at all, and they took me right back. The doctor there wanted to do a pelvic exam right away, and I freaked out!

I said, "Absolutely not! I am not going to go through that just for Dr. Brown to get here and repeat it. No way! Not happening!" .

Austin looked at him and said very calmly, like only Austin can, "She has been through way too much, at this point, to put her through anything that is unnecessary. We will wait for Dr. Brown." That doctor paused, stared at us, but then left the room without a word.

Dr. Brown finally got there. She walked into the room and

asked me to explain again what happened. She said that she doubted that anything was severely torn, but she would have to do a pelvic exam to see. Now, if you remember from my account of the last surgery, there was a damaged area that she repaired. So, the first thing she noticed was the repaired area had been ripped open and was now a fairly large, nasty, bleeding wound. She said that this was probably where I was feeling most of the pain and reassured us that she was sure the vaginal cuff was still intact, but then she did the full pelvic exam.

Austin said that the look on her face told volumes. I was pretty much out of my head in pain. Dr. Brown said that the entire vaginal cuff had ruptured. This meant that the part of the sock that was once closed was now completely ripped wide-open with very frayed, damaged edges. She said I needed to have surgery as soon as they could get the operating room ready.

To be perfectly honest, part of me was relieved. I was relieved because this reassured me this was not in my head! I wasn't just a weak nutjob, and this was not me making something out of nothing. It was not just scar tissue! This was not something that taking some pain medication and sleeping it off would cure. She reassured me that there was a reason I was in extreme pain, but she also made it clear to Austin and I that we had done nothing wrong. I'm pretty confident she was choking down her humble pie and couldn't believe this had happened. If she wasn't choking it down, then she should be—in my humble opinion, that is.

After she left the room to get ready for surgery, Austin and I looked at each other in total shock. I frantically said to him, "Is this really happening? I'm heading into emergency surgery in less than an hour? This is surgery number three—are you kidding me? Who does this happen to? Nobody we know, that's for sure! We have to call some people. Someone else needs to start praying because we need help! On second thought, I don't want anyone to know about this! We can't tell people! What would we say? My insides blew open during intercourse? No way! I can't face this!"

Austin grabbed my hands, looked into my very terrified eyes, and said, "Kennedy, let's pray. We need to try to find some peace, and I only know one thing that can give us that. Can we pray, please? Heavenly Father, we are totally at a loss here. We feel nervous and scared, and we need You to help us. Please protect Kennedy as she endures another surgery. Help her to find comfort. Please, calm her beating heart. Be with Dr. Brown and guide her hands. Be with the girls as they are waking up this morning without us there. You know what we need, and we just ask that You provide that and just stay with us, Father. Amen."

Why was this happening?

God only knows …

Chapter 10

Recovery from Surgery #3

Waking up from this surgery was not fun. It was a lovely spring Sunday afternoon, and I was in the hospital but trying to remember why. The pain was very intense. I remember trying to tell my nurse how much pain I was in. My friend and neighbor, Kate, was in my hospital room with me as Austin had gone home to be with the girls. Right away, I could tell that my nurse, who we will now call Miss Nasty Nurse, was annoyed with me. Actually, it probably had nothing to do with me, and she maybe just hated her job or had tough things going on in her own life. As crazy as it may sound, it appeared that she didn't like it when patients told her they were in pain. The last time I was in the hospital after surgery #2, I had experienced an issue with the pain meds they put directly into my IV. If it was put in too fast, my heart would beat out of control and I had a hard time catching my breath. I also instantly felt nauseous. I don't know if this was a normal reaction, but I do know it was mine, and they wrote in my chart that the medication had to be administered very slowly. On this occasion, Miss Nasty Nurse came in with the meds. Without saying a word and in her very perturbed behavior, she slammed that medication into my IV as fast as she could. My symptoms were instant. I couldn't breathe, my heart raced out of control, and I felt like I might throw up immediately.

Kate jumped up and said, "Oh no, what's going on? What's happening? Are you okay? Oh goodness, not good! Something is not right! Oh dear, oh dear!" She started to get weak in the knees herself.

Miss Nasty Nurse said, "What's the problem?"

While gasping for breath, I said, "Too fast. It says in my chart that those meds have to go in very slowly."

Her response, which I will never forget was, "Do you think I have time to read your chart? You are fine!"

With that, she left the room. I know Kate and I were both in shock. Did that really just happen? What planet are we even on? Oh yeah, the one where crazy things happen that catch you off guard … but I'm really beginning to wonder if the Oliver family has some kind of magnet that attracts events that make you say, "Are you kidding me?" I should have put a disclaimer at the beginning this book. Please be warned, the question, "Are you kidding me?" may seem overused, but after you read you may wonder whether it was used enough!

This situation with Miss Nasty Nurse was in no way a reflection of the kind of care I received from most nurses over the course of this journey. Unfortunately, she was the one I remember. Isn't that always the case? I am a teacher, and I know that all teachers have experienced this. No matter how good a teacher you are, people remember the bad ones and the negative experiences they have had, and they have no problem sharing them. Some people really hang on to that memory and blame all teachers because of it. I'm here to tell you that nurses are amazing people! Miss Nasty Nurse was rare and does not represent all nurses. I could not do the job that they do. Both Austin and I have so much gratitude for the care we received throughout our journey. Nurses are incredible people, and we are thankful for them. They do not receive enough credit, that's for sure! Thankfully, Miss Nasty Nurse is not the norm.

When Lucy and Chloë got to the hospital that day with Austin, they walked into the room looking scared. I tried to put on the best face that I could. I could tell that they really didn't want to get close to me. It was heartbreaking. I wanted to fall apart into an ugly cry puddle, but I needed to be strong for my sweet little girls.

Lucy was the first to come over and give me a hug. "Hi, Mom, are you okay?"

Chloë was next, but very reluctant. She said nothing and gave me the kind of hug you would give to a stranger who made you nervous. Oh, my precious girls! How could we explain this to them when we didn't even really understand it ourselves? What had caused this, and why was this happening to us?

With that, Austin had both girls lie down next to me on the bed. He hugged all three of us and said a prayer. "Heavenly Father, please help us understand why we are going through this. Be with Mom as she begins to heal. Please heal Mom, Father. Help Lucy, Chloë, and I take care of her the best way that we can. We know that You are in control, and we are trusting in that. Amen."

We left the hospital after four days. We were told that I'd had an infection that had made the vaginal cuff weak, and that was why it ruptured. The infection was on the inside, so I had looked healed from the outside when Dr. Brown had given us the okay for all activity. This is how we understood it, and what we were told at the time. Ultimately, we found out months later after combing through my medical records that there was no infection at all. Huh? This made it hard to understand why they'd told us that there was, but it didn't really change anything at that point. When we were released from the hospital this time, it was with strict orders for me to do nothing, lift nothing, and take it very slow. Why didn't any of this make sense?

God only knows …

Chapter 11

Guess Who Was in My Dream?

If I'd felt like I'd been hit by a truck before, it had now turned into a jet engine flying at three hundred miles per hour. I was in rough shape, to say the least. My brother, Jack, had set up a schedule of caregivers to come be with me during the day so that Austin felt okay leaving me when he went to work. They also set up a meal schedule through church so that Austin didn't have to worry about that. Can I just say that people were truly amazing! The generosity of others humbled us beyond measure, and we couldn't have been more grateful! Austin and I are introverts by nature, which is kind of funny, considering we are teachers. Big social scenes are just not in our comfort zone. This stretched us to not only admit we needed help in our home but to accept it.

On the second night home from the hospital, I was feeling depressed. Lucy and Chloë were getting ready to go up to bed, and I was getting very emotional about not being able to climb the stairs to tuck them in. Lucy, who is so perceptive, said to me, "Mom, are you okay?"

"I'm okay, honey. I just feel sad that I can't take you guys up to bed."

"It's okay, Mom, I'll tuck Chloë in for you. I'll tell her to try to sleep all night. I'm really glad that you're home, Mom. Can you promise that there will be no more surgeries?"

"I really want to promise that, Lucy. I'm pretty sure there won't be anymore, so don't worry, honey. I love you, sweet girl!"

"I love you too, Mom!"

That night, I had the most vivid dream. In the dream, I was lying in bed when the doorbell rang. I very slowly got up and went to the door. I opened it, and you are not going to believe who was standing there. It was Oprah! The one and only! She said right away, "Kennedy?" It was as if she recognized me from years ago or something.

"Yes … it's me. I'm Kennedy!" I still couldn't believe she knew my name, but then again, this was my dream.

"I hear you have been very sick lately."

"Yes, it's been kind of rough, that's true."

"Well, Kennedy, you have been chosen to be part of *Oprah's Big Give*! Have you heard of my show?"

I thought, *Are you kidding me? Of course, everyone knows about* Oprah's Big Give! *I can't believe Oprah is at my door and chose me! Things like this don't happen to me! Is she going to send us on a vacation? I would love to go on a vacation! We could really use a vacation! Please make it someplace warm by the beach where we can see dolphins jumping offshore. Oh, and could it be some sort of all-inclusive? We've never been to one of those before, and people rave about them. Beach, sun, sand by the ocean with dolphins jumping—I'm pretty sure I could heal there, and I feel like my people deserve a break from this nightmare life we are living!*

The next thing I knew, Oprah stepped aside to show me what I'd won. She put her arms around this guy as if he was the most precious person on the planet. He appeared to be a tiny Native American man and was wearing a full headdress and everything. By tiny, I mean like under four feet tall … way shorter than Oprah.

I thought, *Huh? Is this really happening? But … I really want to go on a vacation! Are you kidding me?*

"Kennedy, we are giving you a tiny Native American healer! Can you believe it? It's going to be great! This is the first time we've been able to grant such a gift!"

I stood there in shock. Who does this happen to? I get chosen for *Oprah's Big Give*, I receive a little man, and I'm supposed to be grateful for this first-ever gift? What gives? (I couldn't resist.) Does this mean we don't get to go on vacation?"

In my utter disappointment, there seemed to be a long pause and then a beautiful feeling came over me. It's hard to explain. It was like something warm and amazing was behind me. It was a calming presence. I gradually looked over my left shoulder, and I was enveloped in a wonderful, warm, beautiful light. The moment felt like an eternity. One that I never wanted to end. It was a feeling like no other. It was Jesus, and He was hugging me. I was overcome with a sense of peace like I had never felt before. My feeling of upset was gone. I wanted this moment to last forever.

Jesus said to me, "Kennedy, you are going to be okay. This is not just about you—it is something for many people to learn from. I love you, Kennedy!"

I remember waking up with a feeling of calm. I still felt like I had been hit by a jet engine going three hundred miles per hour, but I somehow felt like I could handle it. I would do my best to show my girls what it means to be thankful for all that you have and to cherish those you share it with. I might not be able to run around with them, take them up to bed, or be as active as I would like to be. However, I could show them that even when times are difficult, you can still put your best foot forward and rely on faith to get you through. I was still here, and I had so much to be grateful for. I didn't have to look very far to find somebody who was suffering way worse than me. I had a lot of support, I had an amazing family, and I felt blessed.

"Thank You, Jesus, for this new day and for all that I have. Thank You especially for meeting me in my dream and for giving me peace." Am I really going to be okay?

God only knows ...

Chapter 12

A Long Road of Uncertainty

Let the road to recovery begin. I'm glad that I didn't know how long this road would be, or I might have given up before I started the fight. This would be the beginning of a lot of doctoring without any real answers, and if I'd thought I'd felt nauseous before, now it seemed like it was twenty-four seven. Every time I ate something, I had to fight the urge to run and throw up, and a lot of the time I didn't win. It was horrible! Was it the infection? Wait, there never really was one. Was it my gallbladder? Was this all in my head? All the tests came back negative. I did have a CT scan that showed that I had a very large hiatal hernia that I didn't have prior to my vaginal cuff blowing up. Could this be the cause of the nausea? I also had almost constant bleeding from the wound that wouldn't heal in my area down under. This was from the repair area that had ripped open before the last surgery. On top of that, I felt like I had a million needles inside of me. It was like sitting on a pin cushion. It turned out that this was from all the dissolvable sutures that were used to repair the vaginal cuff rupture. They'd become razor sharp and were stabbing me continuously.

I felt like we were constantly being tested. Our lives also became very isolated. Given that I felt so horrible all the time, we hardly went anywhere, and if we did attend a family gathering or a social event, we didn't stay long. I found that it became very hard to explain to people what was going on because we didn't really know. I developed a phobia of eating in public because I was afraid of the nausea. On more than one occasion, I was questioned by friends and family as to why I wasn't eating.

Some of the many questions I faced were, "Are you going to eat? Why aren't you dishing up? Can I get you a plate? Don't you think eating will make you feel better? Maybe you don't feel good because you aren't eating … maybe that's why you aren't healing."

Oftentimes people were just direct with their suggestions, like, "You have to eat to heal. Just eat, and you'll feel better. You want to get better, don't you? Then you'd better eat!"

I started this journey at 150 pounds and not even a full year later I had lost over 30 pounds. This led to rumors about anorexia. At more than one gathering, there were comments made like "How is your bulimia going for you?" or "How's the anorexia?" Relationships, at times, became more difficult than the actual symptoms. More tears were shed over people's comments, questions, and perceptions than about the actual physical agony. People mean well but can be very cruel at the same time … or maybe those are just the comments that stick with you.

During that summer of 2008, I had a surgery to remove and repair the stabbing sutures, I started to lose my hair in alarming amounts, and I knew that I had to do something about the start of school in the fall. Physically, I knew I couldn't work, but I also knew that we relied on my income to live. At this point, I had been receiving long-term disability, which was a fraction of my salary, and the bills were beginning to mount. Thankfully, we had great insurance, but that certainly didn't cover everything. The financial stress that goes along with an extended illness is very real. Austin and I dealt with it alone and didn't often talk about it with each other, much less with anybody else. There were times during this journey where somebody would suggest to us that we needed more help, but it always seemed like we weren't in a position that was bad enough—does that even make sense? It was only supposed to be six weeks! We did not have an official diagnosis. Nobody knew what was wrong with me, and we honestly thought that I would improve with time.

Doctors were now saying that because of my lack of nutrition, my wounds from the previous surgeries weren't healing. They also said that the nausea was caused by the large hiatal hernia. The next suggestion was that I get that fixed, which would mean another surgery. This was very scary to us. If you get a hiatal hernia fixed, there are things that you cannot do ever again. My understanding was that they would pull the hernia back down and clamp it at the base of my esophagus. This would mean that I could no longer burp, throw up, or drink anything carbonated, among other possible ramifications. Again, this was how we understood it, and it freaked us out! At this point, I was throwing up every single day, sometimes multiple times. We were at a loss as far as what we should do. We really felt like we didn't know where to turn. We were getting advice from many different people, and yet we still felt totally lost. Included among the advice that we were receiving was to get a second opinion at a world-renowned clinic in Minnesota that was about three and a half hours from our home. How would we get through that?

God only knows …

Chapter 13

Fall 2008 and the Long Road
to a Clinic Far Away

Going to a new clinic gave me so much hope, anxiety, and fear. I was afraid because I didn't know what to expect. I had already had some pretty bad experiences with doctors and medical facilities, and I was afraid they were going to be mean and tell me I was crazy. The one thing we found out almost immediately was that things happen fast at this new place. People come there from all over the world, so they do their best to line up appointments and tests within a short time period so that it works for travel plans. I got into the gastroenterology clinic for my hiatal hernia and vomiting issue and also the dermatology clinic for my hair-loss issue pretty quickly. By quickly, I mean, we started the process of sending my records in August, and my first appointments were at the end of October.

Absolutely, the hardest part of going to a place so far away was leaving Lucy and Chloë. They stayed with Anne and Scott, my sister and brother-in-law, which was their home away from home, but it was still not easy. We had started the tradition before leaving for the hospital of making them a chocolate sheet cake, so we kept that going when we began our new journey. Little did we know that we would be making twenty cakes over the course of the next several months. That recipe is forever committed to memory!

One of the first departments we saw was the GI department. I remember being so nervous about telling the story over and over again and getting the allover body rash multiple times. Like clockwork, my rash did not disappoint. I told the whole story to Dr. Charles, the GI doctor. The crazy bleeding that led to a hysterectomy, which led to a more complete hysterectomy, which led to my insides blowing up, which caused a hiatal hernia and the recommendation that I have it fixed. This was also why I looked like I had anorexia and my hair was falling out by the handfuls.

Dr. Charles's first thought was, "I don't think you have a hiatal hernia because it doesn't show up on the CT scan. We will have to do an endoscopy to see what that shows."

He explained that they would sedate me and put a tube down my throat to my stomach to determine what was going on. I told him that I for sure needed to be out for that because I would totally gag and possibly hack up a lung. I also told Dr. Charles that I would like to keep my lungs inside my body because that will make it easier for me to continue breathing. He just stared at me … he really didn't get my sense of humor. He looked at me as if thinking, *This lady who looks very sick is a whack job of the whackiest kind!*

We went for the endoscopy procedure, and I remember waking up from it and asking right way, "Do I have a hiatal hernia?"

I think whoever was with me said, "Most definitely!" but that could have been in my sedated dream.

It wasn't until we met with the Dr. Charles later that we got the official word.

He said to us, "Apparently, your procedure was quite memorable because you threw up on almost everybody in the room.

Your hernia is quite significant. I'm still not sure that is what's causing your nausea. Do you think you could handle having a very small tube down your nose for a twenty-four-hour acid reflux study?"

My response was, "Are you kidding me? Based on your endoscopy report, I can't handle a tube down my throat while I'm asleep. How was I supposed to handle it while I'm awake?"

His response was, "I'm not sure, but are you willing to try?"

"Of course I will try, but I'm not making any promises. Did you know that I sometimes gag while brushing my back teeth? I also gag while I'm eating mashed potatoes, but I think that's a little bit of an irrational fear that the mashed potatoes will expand in my throat and take over my airway so that I might suffocate. I blame my crazy gag reflex on the technician who did my teeth molds back when I was thirteen. To my dismay, she overfilled the tray, stuck the gigantic mold in my mouth, and the cement-like goo immediately started oozing down my throat. I went a little crazy! She kept telling me to calm down. I couldn't get that goo out of my mouth fast enough. I threw up on her too. Can you relate to the teeth-mold thing? Did you have braces?"

A very long awkward paused ensued ... did they not know about the teeth-mold thing? Who doesn't know about the teeth-mold thing? It's a nightmare! Dr. Charles, along with the resident who was with him at the time, just stared blankly at me.

I stopped talking, and Dr. Charles in a very monotone voice said something like, "We have to try to get you to stop doing that—throwing up on people, that is. And, just so you know, I don't know if I could handle it either, so I admire you for trying. This test will be very helpful in determining how much acid from your stomach is coming up, which could be the cause of your nausea."

Off to another appointment at the Clinic Faraway we went.

That will be our new name for it: the Clinic Faraway. Doesn't it sound mysterious and a bit fascinating? Have you ever been to the Clinic Faraway? While feeling like garbage? My guess is if you said yes to the first question, you also said yes to the second, because who goes to the Clinic Faraway unless they feel like total garbage? My point is, everywhere you look you see sick people being led or wheeled by stressed, overtired caregivers. They are all holding a piece of paper that has their all-important schedule on it, which lists all their appointments, tests, and procedures for the week. Everyone looks a little glassy-eyed with some anxiety mixed in.

Anyway, I was so nervous about this tube-down-my-nose thing while being awake that my full-on body rash appeared in full force just sitting in the waiting area before being called back. I asked if Austin could go with me, and the response was no, which made me tear up before I even sat down in the procedure room.

The nurse who does all the tube-down-your nose procedures was very kind. I will call her Kind Tube Nurse. She reassured me immediately that she had never had anyone fail at this because the tube is so tiny, and quite frankly, she was just very good at her job. I don't know if this calmed my fears or made me more anxious. Was I going to be her first ever fail? Was I going to be the cause of her wanting to quit her job that she does amazingly well at? Oh, the pressure! I started the "I *can* do this!" self-talk, and Kind Tube Nurse started to explain how things would go. The goal of this procedure room was to create a place of calm. It had great indirect lighting, lovely calming music, and a very nice leather recliner to relax in, none of which seemed to make a difference to me.

Kind Tube Nurse started to approach my nose with the tube as I lay in the lovely recliner. She got the tube to the back of my throat, and I made a horrible, very loud sound and my insides felt like they were going to start coming out of every hole on my body at umpteen miles per hour. I grabbed the tube and yanked it out of my nose. I know, not a very good first attempt.

She said very calmly, "It's okay. It's okay," in her Kind-Tube-Nurse voice. "Catch your breath, and we'll try again. Remember to keep breathing, Kennedy. This doesn't affect your airway at all. You can still breathe, so try to stay calm. You can do this."

Are you kidding me? That tube was huge! Furthermore, as it started to come toward my nose, it appeared to grow! I attempted to get it down four more times. She even got it almost all the way in on the fifth try, but I was hyperventilating so badly and making horrible sounds like I just might die that she was the one who pulled it out.

She said to me, "Oh dear, I am so sorry. This is just not my day, and I really don't want to keep torturing you."

I started to bawl. I had failed and so had she ... her first time ever!

I came out to the waiting room where Austin was and just started sobbing. It was an ugly cry of the ugliest kind. When I achieved some semblance of composure, I said to Austin, "I flunked the tube-down-your-nose test, and now what are we going to do? I just want to go home! Please take me home! I don't want to go to the hotel! I want to go home ... please! I am over this ... completely over it! Do you hear me?"

Austin knew that I had more appointments to get to over the next couple of days, so going home was not an option. He said nothing. He took my hand, and we walked away from that area very slowly without talking at all. Austin knew this was not a moment to talk but just to hold my hand and lead me out. We made our way down the elevators, through the atrium area where lovely piano music was playing. It was the kind designed to calm everyone's hearts, but all I wanted to do was go over and bang on those black and white keys.

This Clinic Faraway was not small and required a lot of travel within its walls. The comforting and, at the same time, sad part was that we weren't alone in our despair. Many people were there on a similar journey. I say similar, but I truly believe in my heart that we were the only ones in the world walking down this particular road. Our road seemed to be one that was untraveled by anyone. We actually needed a machete to whack down the tall, very thick weeds in our path. Are you getting my drift at all? At any rate, we made it out of the building and back to the parking ramp where the van was parked.

We sat in the van, and Austin prayed, "Father, help us to understand or at least find peace on this road. We are feeling lost and trying to trust in You. Please comfort Kennedy and ease her pain. Amen."

His prayer annoyed me because in my head I was saying, *Really, God? What the hell? None of this makes sense, and why are we even doing this? You have sent us down this path, and You know what? You haven't even given us a damn machete! We are expected to walk through this thick, nasty, very tall brush without even so much as a butter knife to cut down the path. Are you truly kidding me right now?*

While my prayer rant was going on in my head, Austin turned on the van and the radio. This song came on. We didn't even know the radio stations in this city, so Austin just put on a random station. The first song that came on was one that we had never heard before. It was called "Praise You in the Storm" by Casting Crowns. It's about how we surely would have thought that, at this point in our journey, God would have fixed every-thing that was broken. However, since my broken parts aren't yet fixed, we will praise God for them and every other trial we are being faced with.

Do you think this was just by chance? The timing of this song, I mean. Is this just a coincidence? Well, remember my machete woe-is-me thoughts? They did an about face, and I turned my crappy attitude into being grateful … just like that. This is called a miracle, people. You might not think of it like that, but I sure as hell did. You see, I'm a stubborn woman. I get a thought in my head, and I struggle to change it, especially if it's negative. It really takes me a long time—just ask Austin!

I don't know if you are like me at all, but I find it easy to praise God when life is good. Actually, I sometimes even forget to give Him credit. I tend to think I had something to do with it—no joke. You know, when your job is good, your kids are perfect, your marriage is at a peak … that's when God is getting awards from me, or I'm giving myself the awards and maybe telling Him thank you at the dinner table.

However, it's when life is hard and the path you're on calls for a machete—that's when praising Him is so completely filling! To praise God and find gratitude when life has thrown you a boatload of lemons (I'm exaggerating a little bit … we've only been thrown a raft of lemons). Anyway, I think you get what I mean. That's when you know you are not alone and thank goodness for that! Can I get an *amen*, people?

At that moment in the parking ramp of the Clinic Faraway, Austin said, "I think this song was meant for us."

We then leisurely drove around that city. It was a rainy, miserable day, but we felt God's presence. We talked about His plan being greater than ours and how we were going to keep trying to trust in that. We prayed that the girls, the doctors, and the people who were there with us at the Clinic Faraway who were on their own journeys would know His peace. I'm not sure how anyone goes through this life without it.

We went back to see Dr. Charles the next day. He said that he was sorry about the miserable appointment with the Kind Tube Nurse. He again reassured me that he didn't think he could do the test either. His next question was a strange one. He asked if I could eat eggs.

He clarified the question and asked, "Can you eat eggs and keep them down?"

What was he even getting at?

God only knows …

Chapter 14

Celebrating My Birthday and National Mole Day at the Clinic Faraway

The folks at the dermatology clinic were so pleasant. They listened to my story with compassion and attentiveness. They seemed to truly feel bad for what we had gone through and, believe it or not, I didn't even break out into the allover body rash. I was there to see why my hair was falling out. They were totally thorough and did an allover body check. They discovered that my hair follicles looked healthy and that my hair would grow back over time. They said that whenever a person goes through significant trauma, it can cause other unfortunate things to happen. Hair loss is one of those. They suspected that the trauma of having four surgeries with the third one being an emergency due to the vaginal cuff rupturing was enough to cause this significant hair loss.

That was good news that we were happy to receive. On top of that, because of their thoroughness, we found that I had two suspicious moles on my right foot. One was between my third and fourth toes and the other was on the bottom of my foot. This meant that I had to have them removed, which I was sure was going to be a simple procedure. They set up the removal appointment for the next day, which was when we were scheduled to go home. After the mole removal, we would go home until we had to come back for more appointments—the egg eating adventure and the first visit with gynecology. Our plan was to check out of our hotel, kill time around the city, and leave town after that appointment. We were so excited to get home to the girls!

We got to the dermatology clinic early, and thankfully they were able to take me right back. I let Austin wait out in the waiting area and didn't even ask if he could come back. I surely could handle a simple mole removal. I'd had it done before, and it had been a piece of cake. Speaking of cake, this also happened to be my birthday. I know, right? It was October 23, 2008, my birthday, but I discovered that it was also National Mole Day— who knew? I knew that these moles of mine were different from the Mole Day mole (something I should have learned about in Chemistry class), but still, wasn't it a smidge funny? Let the mole removal begin!

Dr. Dole came into the room and asked to see my mole. Isn't it funny that his name was Dole and he wanted to see my mole? Was his best friend Dr. Seuss? Actually, Dole was not his name, but I chose that name for him for this book because it just makes me smile.

Dr. Dole said, "Yes, they definitely need to be removed. Do you know that it's going to require you to be on crutches or off your feet for three to four weeks, Kennedy?"

Wait, what? Did he really just say that?

I questioned, "This isn't just where you use a little liquid nitrogen and scrape them off?"

"Unfortunately, no; this will require us to dig them both out and use stitches to close the areas. Are you okay with us proceeding?"

By the way, I'm pretty sure he didn't use the word *dig* in case you were wondering. *Dig* just sounded better than cut or excise … actually, they are both bad when referring to your own body.

"Can I call Austin and warn him?"

"Sure, of course you can."

I called Austin, who was walking around the Clinic Faraway because Austin is someone who cannot sit still. Like always, his response was very positive. He encouraged me and said he would work on finding some crutches for when we got home.

We didn't call this a surgery even though they took two big huge chunks from between my toes and on the bottom of my foot. We called it my birthday-mole-day procedure, and it was not fun!

I left the Clinic Faraway in a wheelchair that day with many stitches in my right foot, without any real answers as to why I was always nauseous, and I still had a bleeding crotch wound but couldn't get into the gynecology clinic until December. Can I continue to keep doing this?

God only knows …

Chapter 15

In Between Faraway
Appointments and More

The thing about going to a long-distance medical facility is that communication is a bit more complicated, and when we were home in between appointments, we felt alone. We pretty much stopped going to see any of our local medical doctors and put all our hope into the Clinic Faraway. We got home from the foot surgery and failed GI tests and felt totally overwhelmed. I was on crutches, I kept losing weight and hair daily, I was still bleeding from my crotch wound, and I was nauseous all the time. We didn't really have any answers yet, and on top of everything else, the wounds on my foot soon began to open and look really ugly. What was happening? We continually wondered what was going on with my body.

I remember just wanting to crawl into bed and cry, but I had two bright, shining stars named Lucy and Chloë who continually kept my emotions in check. They kept us smiling, laughing, and feeling okay with what life was throwing at us. We made hanging out in Mom and Dad's bed a good time. They camped out with us in our room, did homework in our room, and we made sure it was a room that they wanted to be in. They loved watching *The Brady Bunch*, *7th Heaven*, and any family movie we could get our hands on. If I couldn't make it up to their rooms or out to our family room, then they made sure they brought the party to me.

During this time, Austin was teaching about forty-five minutes away from where we lived. He did an amazing job balancing it all! He would get the girls up and out in the morning, get me what I needed for the day, and then race off to the high school where he taught. He tried, for the most part, to come with me to all my appointments at the Clinic Faraway, but there were a few occasions where it just wasn't possible.

My next set of appointments were all in one day, and it was an extremely exhausting trip. It was difficult and expensive to stay in a hotel, but it was also hard to travel three and a half hours, go to several medical appointments, and then drive home on the same day. I did this while also dealing with a very painful and swollen open foot wound; a nasty, very sore open wound down under; and almost constant nausea. My friend Kate offered to take me to my appointments this time so that Austin didn't have to take more time off from school.

Remember when Dr. Charles asked if I could eat eggs and keep them down? Well, this was the test. In my simple non-medical terms, I will try to explain. I had to eat radioactive eggs and not throw them up over a six-hour period. They would then take pictures at several intervals throughout the day to see how they traveled through my system. The crazy thing was that I got through all the picture taking without throwing up, but I became more and more nauseous as the day went on. Right after they took the last picture, I threw up the eggs.

I remember thinking, *Wow! After six hours, they still kind of look like eggs, just in a mushier form.* Sorry for those lovely details. Just thought you might want to know what my thrown-up eggs looked like.

After that, Kate and I made our way to see Dr. Charles. I remember him watching me get wheeled down the hall. It was late on a Friday afternoon, and I felt guilty thinking we were keeping him from getting to his weekend. He looked at me with pity in his eyes. He said, "Oh no, what happened to you?"

Even though all the doctors were in the same facility, it didn't seem like they communicated with one another. He didn't even know that I'd had a foot procedure on Mole Day. The system was not perfect, that's for sure.

I sat across from him at the appointment, and he read through the results of the egg test. He said that, basically, I had failed it. He said that after so much time, those eggs should have gone through my system. He called my condition gastroparesis. In other words, I had a paralyzed stomach. He said it would explain why I was nauseous all the time. I remember feeling the rash come up my neck as he spoke. I started to sweat, not really knowing what this diagnosis meant.

Dr. Charles said that it was a good thing that I hadn't had the hiatal hernia fixed in Wisconsin. He said that I would have had a real problem on my hands if they had done that surgery. As it stood, food wasn't moving through my stomach, so there would have been nowhere for it to go, and I would have been in a world of hurt or even worse, if you know what I mean.

I remember asking him, "What does this even mean, and why did this happen?"

He didn't really have answers for the why, but he did say that there were medications that could help with this condition. He started me right away on the first one, which caused some bad side effects, and so we eventually went on to the second drug, which helped tremendously. The unfortunate part was that you couldn't get it in the United States. It used to be approved by the drug gods, but they had since taken it off their approval list. I think it had something to do with it not being a big enough moneymaker as other drugs. Don't even get me started because it really makes my blood boil to think about it. We would have to get the meds from other countries and, of course, it wouldn't be covered by insurance. Austin took care of all of it. He tracked it down, ordered it, and made sure that I didn't run out. I did absolutely nothing but take it before I ate and, for the most part, it worked. For the first time in a long time, I felt like we had some answers. Would I have to take this medicine for the rest of my life?

God only knows …

Chapter 16

Financial Worries When
You Are Chronically Ill

Prior to my first surgery, I was teaching at 83 percent time. I started this schedule after Lucy was born. It allowed me to be home with her for an extra hour and a half in the morning, which over the course of one school year is a little more than 285 hours! That's almost twelve more days that I got to spend with my sweet baby girl, and then girls, once Chloë was born. The year Chloë started preschool, I let my principal know that I was ready to go back to full time when the opportunity arose.

Unfortunately, that didn't happen prior to my six-week medical leave. So, when my leave turned into more than anyone expected, I got a call from our business manager at the school district. She explained to me that I had now qualified for short-term disability, which was awesome because I was very worried about what would happen when my sick days ran out. The policy I had would pay 80 percent of my 83 percent salary as long as I qualified. Not good money, but better than no money. The kicker was how to make up for that 20 percent when bills began to mount. Going to the Clinic Faraway was a killer financially. On top of that, in 2008, the gas prices were killers too! This didn't help when making many trips out of state.

There are many challenges while being chronically ill. I don't know how people do it who don't have support. It was hard enough managing the constant pain and nausea, but managing the mounting bills added a very daunting, ugly layer of stress. Austin and I, like many people maybe, avoided the topic until it blew up at us. Now, don't get me wrong, we were extremely blessed to have what we had. We were so fortunate to have our educations and our jobs. But when life threw unexpected trash at us over a long period of time … now that was a struggle! We had great insurance, but it didn't cover everything, and it certainly didn't cover the alternative medicine that we were trying.

I hate that it's called alternative, as if it was the wrong way or the path that wasn't the best. The care I received from my chiropractor, healing-touch person, acupuncturist, and psychotherapist was for my whole person. What I mean by that is they looked at everything, not just the mole between my toes and or the ulcer in my crotch. My hope is that someday all therapies, Western, Eastern, Northern, Southern, and even Dr. Seuss will come together and work as one. I wish Western medicine would acknowledge the gifts that Eastern medicine can bring to the person and vice versa.

No matter how you look at it, sickness is stressful. Qualifying for disability was also *very* stressful. I can't imagine how a really sick person jumps through all the crazy hoops. To be unwell and expected to fight for what you have paid for is very difficult. I was an absolutely sick person, but I had a lot of people helping me to jump through those hoops. I think, unfortunately, the goal of the disability insurance company was to bank on the fact that a certain percentage of people would just give up or not even attempt the hoop jumping and then they wouldn't have to pay.

On one special day, I remember getting a call from the financial office of one of our doctors. They said that our insurance was maxed and everything would now be coming out of our pockets, which were empty. Not to mention that our bill from them was thousands of dollars at this point. On that very same day, I got a call from a very nasty case manager from the disability office. I'll call her Mean Case Girl.

Mean Case Girl said to me when I answered the phone, "Kennedy, I'm calling to let you know that you no longer qualify for disability."

My response was, "Excuse me? Nothing has changed for me health-wise. How can that be? I know that my doctor just sent the latest paperwork and said I would have no trouble qualifying. Do you know that I've lost over thirty pounds, I still throw up daily, and my crotch is bleeding constantly?"

Mean Case Girl came back with, "That's unfortunate, but we can't just take a doctor's note. Sorry."

If they can't take a doctor's note, then whose note do they take? Are you kidding me? I got off the phone with Mean Case Girl and fell to the floor sobbing.

"Really God? Are you kidding me? Is this all part of the rotten joke I am living? I'm ready for the punchline! We are behind on bills, we owe several people, and now we're losing my income? What are we going to do?"

God only knows …

Chapter 17

Meeting the GYN at the Clinic Faraway

After finding out why I was having constant nausea, our new prayer was to find out why I had constant pelvic pain and a bleeding, ulcerated area that would not heal. We were very hopeful that the gynecology department at the Clinic Faraway would have some answers for us. I remember praying before the appointment that the doctor would be nice and competent all at the same time. I would soon discover that only one of those two attributes were part of her make-up. She acknowledged that I had a nasty bleeding area but couldn't really explain why. She recommended that I try physical therapy and, just like that, the appointment was over.

I felt like we had been waiting months to get some answers, and in a matter of minutes we were told to try physical therapy. Huh? I couldn't wrap my brain around the fact that physical therapy would be a solution. I got that it could probably help with the pelvic pain, but how was I going to do pelvic exercises while I had a bleeding ulcer? However, like many suggestions along this road that didn't really lead to healing, I was willing to try this one.

Our first meeting with the pelvic specialist was very positive.

She was totally compassionate, understanding, and shocked at what we had already gone through.

She did an exam and immediately said, "Whoa, this looks painful! I'm not sure how the exercises will affect this, but let's see if they can help with the pain."

She went through a routine for me to try, we set up another appointment for two days later, and she sent us on our way.

Let me just remind you that when we went to the Clinic Faraway, we were there for three to four days and packed in many appointments. Usually, Austin and I traveled alone and left the girls with Anne and Scott. On this particular occasion, we brought Lucy and Chloë with us. They hung out with Austin in the waiting area while I went into the various appointments. The girls were thrilled to get to go along. The hotel we stayed in this time had a pool, which they loved, and just the fact that we didn't have to be separated was pure joy.

However, this trip wasn't without its traumatic experience. Because I was becoming very weak and still had open wounds on my foot, I rode in a wheelchair while traveling around the clinic. Lucy and Chloë liked to take turns pushing me, which was a little scary because they were only seven and five at this point, and if you've ever walked around the Clinic Faraway, you know that its equivalent is a Los Angeles freeway during rush hour. You need patience and a good driver if you are in a wheelchair. The girls did a great job while Austin helped direct so we didn't run into too many people or walls.

As we were heading back to the hotel for the day, we traveled down the long hallway to the elevators that would take us to the parking ramp and the van. I remember that there were not any other people in the hallway at the time, which was unheard of in our previous trips. Full of joy, like only children can display during tough times, Lucy and Chloë took off running ahead of us. It was such a treat to see them skipping and giggling as

they went. Just as Austin and I caught up to them at the elevators, Austin stopped the wheelchair and went over to the water
fountain to get a drink. It all happened so fast, but the elevator
doors opened, the girls ran in, and the doors closed. I sat there
in shock. All we could hear were piercing screams.

My heart raced, and I yelled to Austin, "You have to run
up the stairs and catch them before they get out onto the busy
street." There were several floors, and who knows what they
would do or if they would get off?

I remember praying, "Please, God, calm their sweet little
hearts and help them to know what to do. Please don't let them
get out at the busy street!"

I sat in front of those elevator doors for what seemed like
forever. I could still hear Chloë screaming that terrified shrill
scream. Austin came back down the stairs and said that he
couldn't find them. Are you kidding me? Why is our life so
messed up, Lord?

My response was, "You have to! They have been through
too much to now have to be traumatized by a stupid elevator
and getting lost!"

Austin tried to give me the everything-is-going-to-be-all-
right look, but I wasn't having it! I'm pretty sure you could have
seen my heart pounding.

Austin was just about to go back up the stairs when the
elevator doors opened, and there stood our crying girls with a
complete stranger. They ran to me. The man said that they had
gotten out at the crazy busy street level, and they were both
crying. He told them that he would help them find us and got
back onto the elevator with them. We thanked him for helping
us and then paused to have a family hug while all four of us shed
a tear or two and a prayer.

Unfortunately, this ongoing journey had taken a toll on all
four of us. I was the one with the most significant health issues,

but Austin and the girls were just as exhausted. The emotional suffering a person endures when a loved one is chronically ill is very real. There are times, like the elevator incident, which might not seem very traumatic on paper, but are enough to push a person over the edge. It's times like that when you realize what's most important, and that is being together. To this day, whenever we mention the Clinic Farawy, the girls can go right back to that specific event and it's not a very fun memory. They have no desire to ever go back. What were we all supposed to learn from this?

God only knows …

Chapter 18

Surgery at the Clinic Faraway

As a result of my unsuccessful attempts at physical therapy, the pelvic specialist said that I needed to see one of their gynecological surgeons about getting my vaginal mess repaired. Let me remind you that, yes, vaginal mess is a highly technical term, so I hope you can understand what I'm talking about. Unfortunately, you can't just go see a surgeon without a referral from a doctor. This meant that I needed to return to the GYN clinic to see the mean GYN doctor so that she could refer me to a surgeon. I did that, and I survived—I even came out of the appointment rashless. She did not hesitate at all. I feel like we were just following some weird protocol of attempting to fix it with physical therapy, knowing full well that there was no way that would fix it. That's just my humble, uneducated opinion.

Upon meeting with Dr. Dip, the GYN surgeon, we of course had to go through the entire story with him and all his people. Did it get any easier the more I told it? Absolutely not, but I got through it. Was his name really Dr. Dip? Of course not, but he did live up to that name.

After a thorough and painful examination, his recommendation was for me to have a vestibulectomy for the nonhealing vulval vaginal fissure. In layman's terms, this meant they would cut out the area that was a mess while trying not to create more of a mess. I know, it's hard to understand my medical jargon, but please try to hang in there with me. It's also a little bit challenging to write about my parts down under, and I'm kind of getting a rash while I write, so I can assure you that my job of writing is way more difficult than your job of reading.

The vestibulectomy was scheduled for a few weeks down the road, which put us at the beginning of 2009. Yes, we had gone through one more holiday season with this adventure that was only supposed to take six weeks! This would be an outpatient surgery, which meant that Austin and I would stay in a hotel the night before the surgery, but then drive home after I was released from the hospital that afternoon. Our thought was that it would be easier driving home while I was still heavily medicated than it would be staying in a hotel another night and driving home the next day. It also meant that we would only have to pay for one night, which was a plus considering we were not doing very well financially. Furthermore, it would also mean that we would only have to be away from Lucy and Chloë for one night.

The surgery came and went and was deemed a complete success! I would soon be well on the road to recovery because my stomach, although still paralyzed, was starting to function because I had medication that allowed me to eat and now my ulcerated area down under would be all fixed too. Hallelujah! Can I get an *amen*?

Not so fast, people! Driving home was a nightmare, but I survived. Put it this way: it's not easy to ride for three and a half hours on a surgically repaired vagina. I wished that if someone was going to have surgery at a place called the Clinic Faraway, at the very least, you should be able to get a ride home on a beautiful magic carpet. This was certainly not the case. It all makes sense since there really is no such place called the Clinic Farawy with magic carpet taxis in reality.

The first night home, I lay in bed, snuggled with my girlies, and enjoyed a very cold ice pack. However, by the next morning, the pain was so intense that I was kind of out of my head, and the bleeding was pretty bad too. Was this normal? Who knew, but it was very hard to recover so far away from where I'd just had surgery. Austin made many calls back to the clinic, but we didn't get many reassurances and were too many hours away to be seen. So, we finally called one of our GYN friends near where we lived. Dr. Kathryn Smith made some calls for us and got us in to see a gynecologist that she knew. We couldn't go see Kathryn because she now worked for the university and only saw students and faculty, but she sent us to someone who would become one of our most trusted doctors and friends.

Little did we know that our first meeting with Dr. Stephen Hopkinson would be the beginning of a very long relationship. He promised not to ditch us at that very first appointment, and he certainly kept his promise. Would we have kept going had we known that additional nightmares lay ahead?

God only knows ...

Chapter 19

Dr. Steve and the End of
the Clinic Faraway

I think that Dr. Hopkinson, or Dr. Steve, as we now call him, is my age. However, when he walked into the room at that first meeting, I thought, *Oh no, he looks like he just got out of school!*

At the time, I didn't really care though, because I was in so much pain! Dr. Kathryn had given him some information about us, but we still had to go over the whole story. It helped me to have Austin there. I remember the exam part was a nightmare because I was in such total pain.

I'm pretty sure Dr. Steve's impression of me at that very first meeting was *Oh no, what is wrong with this woman, and what am I in for? She's kind of a nutjob!*

I'm also pretty sure had Steve known what the long road ahead would look like, he might not have agreed to see us in the first place. Thankfully, our GYN friend, Kathryn, had told Steve that we were not nutjobs but instead normal people who had been down a very crazy, unexplainable road.

Dr. Steve helped us manage the pain and said that he would continue to see us as needed since the road to the Clinic Faraway was a long one. However, we did continue to go back and forth thinking that the surgeon we had there would help us through the recovery process. I remember during one post-op appointment with the doctor at the Clinic Faraway, I explained that I had one area that was still very sore and bleeding on a continual basis. At the time, Dr. Dip was in the room along with his nurse as well as Austin. He started asking me questions about what kind of activity I had been doing. I told him that I was doing literally nothing. It hurt to sit, so I spent most of my time lying down.

His response was, "There's your problem. You should be able to do anything you want. If that's riding a bike, go do it! If you want to have sex, go for it!"

Austin and I were kind of shocked, and Dr. Dip's nurse, who was standing behind him, was shaking her head, "No way!"

He then did an exam, and I thought I would go out of my mind. He was rough, it hurt like you know what, and I thought for sure I was going to throw up!

I remember him saying something like, "Oh, I guess maybe you might need a little more time before you get on that bike. How long ago was your surgery?"

At that point, it had been six weeks, so he said to give it a couple of more weeks and then I'd be good to go.

I asked, "So the area that is very raw and still bleeding—that will heal in a couple of weeks?"

His response was, "Sure, you'll be fine. Anything else we can do for you?"

Before leaving the clinic that day, Dr. Dip's nurse apologized and said that I definitely needed to take it easy. Austin and I left feeling so alone with all of it. We had seen doctors who blew us off back home, and now we felt like we were being blown off again. Nobody could tell us why the area would not heal or why I was in so much pain. We felt very defeated, to say the least, and although we had gotten some answers about my stomach and we now had medicine to help with that, I was still throwing up several times a week as the medicine did not help 100 percent of the time. On top of that, I struggled to take any kind of pain medicine because it added to the nausea.

We got home from that particular trip to the Clinic Faraway and I told Austin, "I quit. I'm done with doctors, and we are just going to live like this. I'm sick and tired of people who don't have a clue and who don't really care! I have a crotch that bleeds and hurts like crazy to sit on. Like I'm ever going to be able to ride a bike or do anything ever again! I still feel like I have needles between my toes, my foot isn't healing right, and I have a stomach that is paralyzed. Oh, and I'm still nauseous most of the time! And in case you haven't noticed, I have a really bad attitude! I quit!"

Austin took me right home when we got into town. He said that he would go get the girls from my sister's house after I got settled. We walked into our house where there was calming music playing, there were uplifting notes everywhere, and there was just a peace and calm that God knew I needed. Austin walked me into the bedroom and helped me lie down.

He said, "Apparently, God knew what we needed to come home to. He gave that message to someone, and they listened to Him." God really is cool like that! My mom, my sister Joy, and my niece Marie are too. They knew we needed to arrive home to peace and tranquility.

Austin brought the girls home, and they snuggled right into bed with me. Lucy was on my right and Chloë on my left. Austin made a pizza for them, and we had a party in our bed.

Lucy asked, "Mom, do you have to go back to the Clinic Faraway anymore?" Austin waited for my answer.

"I don't know, honey. Probably not as much as we've been going. Maybe just a couple more times. I think that our new doctor down here, Dr. Steve is his name, might be able to help us. Would you like it if we didn't go so much?"

Lucy answered, "I just want you to feel better, Mom."

Chloë chimed in, "And we're getting tired of chocolate sheet cake!"

Had we worn out our welcome at the Clinic Faraway?

God only knows …

Chapter 20

Surgery with Dr. Steve and
Many More Doctor Visits

At this point in our journey, my symptoms included nausea with occasional vomiting, gallbladder attacks, nonhealing vaginal bleeding, a very nasty ulcer with pelvic pain, chest pain, brain zaps, and total exhaustion. Some of those symptoms I haven't mentioned previously just because they didn't all make the cut. The cut while initially writing this book, that is.

For example, I would describe the brain zaps as a lightning-bolt feeling that occurred on the left side of my brain. It was a stop-you-in-your-tracks kind of pain that maybe lasted a few seconds and was sometimes accompanied by very lovely facial numbness. We did see a neurologist at the Clinic Faraway for this who was a complete and total jerk. He basically said that they were migraines and that I should feel fortunate that they only lasted a second and to stop wasting his valuable time with something so minor.

I wanted to dropkick him from here to China, which I think I could have done given that I am an excellent punter. I often told my students—when I was teaching, that is—that if I hadn't become a high school math teacher then I certainly would have become a punter in the NFL. Not to brag too much or anything, but I am pretty good. Back in the day, I remember being jealous of my brother who got to participate in the punt pass and kick contest where no girls were allowed. I knew I could have won the punting part. At any rate, I had a lot of very horrible symptoms that were very debilitating and, on top of it, nobody could figure out why.

After I went on my rant to Austin about quitting, I came to my senses and went back to see Dr. Steve.

He did another exam and said, "I am pretty sure I can fix this. I know that you don't want to go back to the operating room, but I think this should be a fairly easy fix."

Austin and I decided once again that this was worth a try. We knew that this vaginal ulcer was causing me a lot of discomfort and that I really would like to be able to sit comfortably in the future, so we agreed to another surgery. This would be the first surgery with Dr. Steve, but the seventh or eighth overall, if you count the National Mole Day surgery.

We had the surgery, and within a few days of being home, it opened up and ultimately did not heal. The wound even got a little bigger, and I would say a tad more painful. What is a tad anyway? One definition is "a small or insignificant amount," so I guess "tad" was not exactly the word that I was looking for. Synonyms for a tad are "bit, whit, mite, touch, modicum, iota, hint, soupçon, fraction," which are all not quite what I was looking for either. Does this even matter? Not really. What matters was that the surgery didn't work, I was in a tad-plus more pain, and this journey was not fun. Yes, this was a totally sucky and not fun road, and six weeks had turned into an eighteen-month journey!

Given that I was still in a boatload of pain, Dr. Steve suggested that I go see some other doctors for possible answers. The first doctor he sent me to was Dr. Evil. He was an "expert" in the gynecological field, so he might have some ideas for us. Thankfully, Austin went with me and sat in on the appointment.

Dr. Evil, after a very rough, painful pelvic examination, said, "Have you thought about wearing mittens to bed? You are obviously doing this to yourself in the night while you are sleeping."

You have got to be kidding me! If I thought about drop-kicking the Clinic Faraway neurologist from here to China, then I definitely wanted to dropkick this butthole right off of the planet. He was not simply a "butt," but a complete and total "butthole." He was the part of the hole that … I think you know what I mean.

Dr. Steve did apologize for sending us there and said very calmly, "Well, at least we've checked him off the list."

We also went to see a dermatologist, a rheumatologist, and a meteorologist. The dermatologist thought it might be lichen planus, but then that was ruled out. According to Wikipedia, "Lichen planus is a chronic inflammatory disease of the skin, mucous membranes, and nails." The rheumatologist ruled out every disease known to humankind, but he was very nice and acknowledged that we had a mess on our hands. He said, "You need to find somebody who's good at cleaning up messes." We liked him, but really? How do you find someone like that? Finally, the meteorologist said that it was going to continue raining on us for a few more years. Actually, we skipped the appointment with the meteorologist because they are wrong a lot of the time anyway. Sorry, I couldn't resist.

Have I mentioned that I wanted to be a meteorologist when I first got to college? Thankfully, I changed directions because I really do love teaching, and I also love high-school-age kids. In addition, I'm not a big fan of thunderstorms or severe weather. Just ask my sister Lee—we have each other on speed dial and call if there is a hint of a storm. For some reason, given that we both are nervous storm nellies, we find comfort in freaking out together about it. The rest of our siblings just laugh at us.

Wow, I'm good at digressing … it's a gift. At any rate, this led us back to Dr. Steve. We had ruled out a lot and narrowed in on nothing. He explained to us that he had one more idea up his sleeve, but that it involved surgery, and it was a hint more serious. He said that one of his partners at the clinic would assist with the surgery and that they thought it could work. Now, given my very expert knowledge of the medical terminology, I will attempt to explain this surgery to you so that you might understand. Their plan was to take a flap of muscle from the right side of my vagina and cover the ulcer, which was at the back side of my vagina, with it. Who knew that this book would use the word *vagina* so many times? Does that bother you? Too bad if it does. What bothers me is that it's my vagina that we've been talking about!

The lovely flap-moving surgery was planned for my birthday, October 23, 2009. We thought, "Oh well, why not give it a try!" Maybe having the surgery on my birthday would bring with it a very special gift of healing or just some extra special luck, not that we believe in that. Well, it did bring a very special gift, but, unfortunately, it was not in the healing department. What other gifts would the birthday surgery bring us?

God only knows …

Chapter 21

The Hema-Son-of-a-Bitch-
Toma from Hell

What I am about to describe is very horrible, to say the least. I can still remember waking up after this surgery. Oh goodness, the pain was intense immediately. This was a new thing because usually the drugs made waking up an experience that had very little feeling associated with it except maybe extreme exhaustion. This was surgery #8 in just under two years' time. Well, actually #9, if you count ... oh goodness, why keep counting? I'm a math teacher. I enjoy keeping count! At any rate, I was lying on my back, the nurse was close by, and I was very uncomfortable. There was this intense pain/pressure between my legs that was indescribable. Ugh! I kept asking her for more pain medicine, which is not something I usually do because it causes me to be nauseous—that tells you how much it hurt!

They got me up to my room, and I remember all the decorations! Woohoo, it was a party!

The person who wheeled me in said, "Wait a minute, it's your birthday? It's a birthday surgery? Oh my, happy birthday?"

She said it like it was a question. Kind of like, "Are you

serious? This really is rotten that you are doing this on your birthday!"

All I remember after that was wanting painkillers for my birthday. The kind of meds that makes you say, "Okay now, that's what I'm talking about!"

So far, that kind of med did not exist in my experience … it was just something I fantasized about.

The next thing I remember was Dr. Stephen Hopkinson entering the room. I am writing out his full name because this event warrants that.

Dr. Steve exchanged pleasantries with Austin, and then looked at me and said, "How's it going?"

That's what Steve says every time he first sees me. It's as if we are friends who pass each other in the grocery aisle. However, we are not in the grocery aisle. In fact, I've never seen Steve anywhere but in his clinic or in the hospital.

After we got past my probable smart-ass response to Steve's, "How's it going?" he said, "Can I take a look?"

He pulled back the coverings, and his eyes got huge. I looked at Austin, whose eyebrows were raised, and his face looked like he was seeing the most hellish thing imaginable.

I started saying, "What? Come on, what is causing your eyes to bulge out of your head and Austin's face to freak out? Hello! What the heck is going on?"

They both just stared in horror. It was definitely not good and made my heart pause momentarily.

Steve finally said, "It looks like you have a hematoma. Can you excuse me for a second?"

"Huh? No, I can't excuse you. What does that even mean? What's a hematoma? I'm guessing it's not a good thing?"

I started to shake. That uncontrollable shake … yes, like after you've had a C-section, that kind of shake. If you're a woman who has had a C-section, you know what I mean. There seems to be no way to stop from shaking.

Steve said, "We might need to go back to the OR."

Steve was calm, but I could tell in his head he was saying, *You have got to be f-ing kidding me! How on earth did this happen?*

He explained that somehow I had a blood vessel that was bleeding inside near the surgical site. This is a common complication after surgery. He told me that it was going to be okay, and he left the room. He said that he would be right back. Maybe he went to throw up. Maybe he went to get a cold compress for his forehead. Actually, I think he went to call his partner who assisted in the surgery. I did wonder if he really would come back. If there ever was a time to ditch, this might have been a good one!

I said to my husband, "Please tell me, is it really bad? Your face looked like it was really bad." Steve's face looked like he saw a ghost. I mean a really disgusting, ugly ghost, if that's even a thing? "What does this mean, Austin? I can't go back to surgery tonight. Please tell me this is not really happening right now. Hello! I'm really freaking out here!"

Austin really had no words. He tried to reassure me, but he wasn't very convincing. He did say that it seemed very large and that he could totally understand why I was in so much pain. Even my always-positive husband couldn't come up with anything on the plus side of things. Are you kidding me?

Steve came back into the room and explained what was going on. He said that somehow I'd had a fairly significant interior bleed. He was not sure when or how it had happened; nonetheless, it had. He said that they thought it would be best to let the hematoma decrease over time and let my body absorb it naturally. We would not be going back to the operating room tonight.

I responded with, "What does this even mean? How much time are we talking about? How long will it take for it to go down, and do you remember my body? It is not capable of doing anything naturally or normally, for that matter!"

Steve wouldn't really commit to a time period, but he implied that it would take a while for my body to reabsorb the blood. He told me to hang in there.

That night, Austin sent out an APB to our support group. For us, APB stands for "All Prayers Begin," which meant that anyone who has ever thought about praying, ever prayed for anything at any time, or anyone who has even made a wish upon a star, we want you to begin praying now! We did not have time for a hematoma—especially a hema-son-of-a-bitch-toma! My get-back-to-work clock was ticking! We'd been notified by the school district that I would lose my job as a teacher if I didn't get back to work by the beginning of second semester. The district was being very generous because, technically, I should have returned to work by mid-November, which would have marked exactly two years since surgery #1.

Oh yeah, and did I fail to mention earlier that Austin had retired from his teaching position at the end of last school year? Taking care of me became his main priority, and we knew that Austin could do other work if needed, but he needed the flexibility to help with my care. So, it was imperative that I got back to work because I carried the health insurance, and we also didn't want to lose our house.

The morning after surgery, they took out the catheter and said that I could get up and take a shower. I hadn't seen the hematoma yet. I knew that it really hurt and that it felt like I had some kind of huge object between my legs that felt like it could explode, but I had not been able to look at it. The nurse helped me into the bathroom and asked if I needed help showering.

I, of course, said, "No, I'm good."

She left the room, and I stood there in front of the mirror. I'm not going to lie. It was something out of a horror movie. It looked like I had a reddish/purplish/bluish football between my legs. It was huge and totally scary! I mean, it was the size of a small football, but when you put it between your legs and it's not really a football, well, that's no longer very small!

I got into the shower, and the blood began to drip. At first it was a drip, drip, drip, and then it started to really flow. Blood was literally pouring down my legs. My vision started to go blurry and it was like I was starting to float. I tried to reach for the cord that alerts the angels that I'm coming to heaven, but it was just out of my reach.

I kept telling myself, "Don't look down. Stop looking at all the blood. Reach for the cord. You can do it! Dear God, please send me an angel now!"

With that last prayer, I felt an angel's arms around me holding me tightly. I looked up into his face.

I said, "Hi, honey. I've been praying for you to come. I'm kind of in a really bad place right now, and I need help."

Austin stayed very calm and held me upright.

He said, "Why are you trying to do this by yourself?"

A nurse then entered the room and said, "Oh goodness, Kennedy. You should have called for help."

Even in that crazy, blood-filled, very painful moment, I was saying to myself, *No shit, Sherlock! You never should have left me in the first place! Everyone knows that when I say, "I'm good," it really means, "I need help!"* They were able to dry me off, get me back into bed, and get me some pain meds. I was originally scheduled to go home that day. Yeah, that didn't happen. Would I survive the natural absorption of the hema-son-of-a-bitch-toma?

God only knows …

Chapter 22

A Very Bad Day That Includes No Underwear, the Swine Flu, and Parent-Teacher Conferences

After three nights in the hospital, it was time for me to take my hema-son-of-a-bitch-toma and blow the joint. Kind of like the saying, "I'm going to take my ball and get the hell out of here." Unfortunately, I really was, and my ball was attached to my body ... for real! I can't even believe I'm writing this! Are you kidding me?

Did I mention that while I was in the hospital, the transmission went out on our van? Austin arranged for it to be fixed through an auto class at a local tech school to save us some money, but it meant that the van would be gone for a few weeks. It didn't really matter to me because I wasn't driving anywhere, but it did mean that I had to try to hoist myself up into our pickup truck, which was no easy feat since I was carrying a rather heavy blood-filled football between my legs. Furthermore, sitting on top of my fancy football was excruciating, especially in a truck that did not have very forgiving shock absorbers.

Coming home to my sweet girls was always something that lifted my spirits. However, Austin warned me that Chloë was home from school early and was at Anne's house because she was under the weather. Austin helped me out of the truck and into the house. He practically had to carry me to the bedroom. He helped me to get out of his sweats because there was no way my fancy football would have fit into mine. There was also no way that I could comfortably wear underwear. I'm telling you, this thing was f-ing huge! We also had to put a large pad under me because I was still bleeding quite a bit from the surgery site.

After lying down and trying to find a comfortable position, I could hear my girlies coming in through the garage door.

"Mom? Are you home?" Lucy yelled.

It was great hearing her voice.

I called back to her in my weak-but-I'm-still-strong-for-you voice, "I'm in here. Hurry!"

"Why do we have to hurry, Mom?"

"Because I can't wait to give you a hug!"

Immediately after giving me a hug, Lucy said, "Are you okay? No more surgeries, right? Mom, did you know that Chloë is sick? What if it's the swine flu, Mom? Did you know that a lot of people have that? They might even close the school. Did you know that, Mom? Dad says she has a fever. He's checking it right now. She doesn't look good at all! She has been crying a lot. Are you okay, Mom?"

Just seeing Lucy lifted my spirits, but she was talking a mile a minute and full of questions.

I said to Lucy, "I want to see Chloë. Can you tell her to come in here?"

I then looked toward the bedroom door, and there stood my sweet little six-year-old. She was as white as a ghost and looked as if she could fall to the floor at a gentle breeze.

"Oh, no. Come here, Chloë-girl."

She walked over and climbed right in beside me. She was burning up!

Austin came in and said, "She has a temp of one hundred and two. She shouldn't really be by you because we don't want you getting what she has."

Are you kidding me? Let the nightmare continue. All I wanted to do was hold my sick baby. Chloë started to cry and so did I.

"Dear God, please help us. We are falling apart here. Please? We need help now!"

On top of all of it, Austin said, "Do you know what tonight is? It's parent-teacher conference night for Chloë. I'm going to call someone to come over and be with you while I go to the conference."

You could see the utter exhaustion on Austin's face. He was doing a great job of holding us all together, but it was definitely wearing on him. The next thing we knew, you could hear someone coming in the door.

We heard her yell from the kitchen, "Hello! It's Joy to the rescue!"

Wow, God, You sure answered that prayer fast! Impressive!

"We're all in here!" Austin yelled.

"How is Team Oliver doing? Oh goodness, half of you don't look very good."

Lucy chimed in talking very fast because it was almost as if she didn't, she might break down crying too. She said, "Mom just got home from the hospital, and she is still bleeding and her body hurts a lot! She says she's okay, but I don't think so. Chloë has the swine flu we think, and she has a very high temperature. A lot of people at school have it … did you know that, Joy? They said they might even close the school. Oh, and Dad just realized that he has to go to Chloë's parent-teacher conference tonight. Dad said he was going to call someone to be with us, and then Mom just prayed for God to help us, and then you walked in. Isn't that amazing?"

"Wow, you Olivers have had a busy day! I'm here for you, so Luc, why don't you and I get supper ready? Sound like a good plan?"

"That sounds good. I would really just like a pizza. Do you know how to make that? It's my favorite. If you don't know how, that's okay. We can have whatever. Chloë should probably have soup, but I don't know if we have soup. Actually, I don't know if she will even eat anything because Anne tried to get her to drink water and she just cried. I guess we should just see if we have pizza. Should we just go check? C'mon, I'll help. It's really amazing how you just came right after Mom prayed. Don't you think?"

Joy replied, "Wow, Luc, it is amazing, and you sure are good at taking care of things!"

Lucy said, "Thanks! You should see my dad—he's really good at it too!"

Austin gave Chloë some medicine and then left for the parent-teacher conference. Joy and Lucy made supper while I just laid in bed with my very huge hema-son-of-a-bitch-toma.

I said a prayer to God while I laid there. "God? I'm not sure what You are thinking. We are really struggling here. Please give us some of Your healing power. You can do it, God. Why doesn't it seem like You want to? Please just help my little girl. We're asking straight up and specific, heal us now! I'm begging, God. Also, about this parent-teacher conference. Can You make it a good one? Lucy struggles enough in school. Please don't make it Chloë too. We are really at a loss here, and we just need some peace … with all of it. Please?"

Austin walked in the bedroom after the conference. Joy was sitting in the recliner holding Chloë, who was sleeping. Lucy was already in bed. He took Chloë up to bed and thanked my sister for answering God's call and helping us out. One thing we have learned through this process is how fortunate we are with the people in our lives. It's humbling beyond words how people just drop what they are doing to come and help us.

After Joy left, Austin came back into the bedroom and said, "Well …" He paused for a long time, and with tears in his eyes, he said, "It's Chloë too. She can't read either. She's in the lowest group for everything … just like Lucy. They suggested that we put her in a special reading class."

Why couldn't our girls learn? What was going on? We knew that Lucy really struggled, and we'd gotten a tutor for her every summer. We also had my mom work with her during the school year. Austin and I were teachers, and yet we couldn't seem to teach our own children. We were totally open to getting them tested for learning disabilities, but given that they were only in third and first grades, their teachers weren't ready to do that. It was so hard to see them have such difficulties.

My heart felt so heavy that night, and sleep was nearly impossible. Austin tried to encourage me to focus on my health. He kept reassuring me that we had beautiful, healthy little girls, and just because they had learning issues didn't mean they wouldn't be successful at whatever they put their minds to.

Austin's prayer that night was, "Heavenly Father, Your plan is perfect, and we are trying very hard to trust in that. Please help us with that. We are asking for healing for Kennedy. Ease her pain. We ask for prayers for Chloë. Please help her to get over whatever this nasty bug is. We really need to get healthy here, and we know that You can do that for us. Thank You, Father, for the people You have put in our lives. We are so humbled by the generosity of so many. We pray these things in Your name. Amen."

Can things get any worse?

God only knows …

Chapter 23

Surgery Number ... Who Really Cares?

With each new day after surgery, I was faced with increased pain and incredible pressure down under. The day after getting home from the hospital, we went back into the clinic where the doctor who assisted Dr. Hopkinson in the operating room tried to evacuate the hematoma. Sorry for the gory details, but this means he cut into it and pressed on it with all his strength. This was all done while I just lay there. No numbing, no meds, nothing—I was out of my head in excruciating pain.

Prior to the procedure, he'd said that he'd thought I would feel instant relief and that the blood would flow out. I imagined it would be like if you've ever slammed your finger in a car door or hit your thumb with a hammer. Do you know what the pressure under your fingernail feels like? It's horrible! The minute that pressure is released, whether you puncture the fingernail yourself or it's done at the doctor, the relief you feel is incredible! Now, let's take that pain and pressure and multiply it by one hundred and then ... you get to experience that down under! That's what I was feeling and what I was expecting to feel when the pressure was released.

As the doctor was pressing like crazy on this hematoma, nothing came out. Not one drop of blood. It was a solid mass of hardened blood. This nightmare procedure provided no relief at all! The excruciating pain I felt actually increased. Just imagine this, on your own body, in a place where the sun doesn't shine. If you are reading this right now and you are a man, can you imagine a very large hematoma there? I'm pretty sure you wouldn't survive. You probably wouldn't have even left the hospital with an extra football attached to your other balls. I'm just trying to get you to feel my extreme pain. Is it working?

Austin and I probably should have demanded that we go back to the hospital right then and there, but we were so utterly exhausted at that point that we didn't even know that was an option. When the office procedure failed, what did we do? I pulled up my pants, with Austin's help, of course, and to be honest, they were his pants because my lovely football wouldn't fit into mine. We headed back home. I was in more pain than when we went in. We were told that my body would have to reabsorb the blood over time, and we're not talking days. This was going to be months!

We called the doctor on call from Dr. Steve's clinic every night. I'm pretty sure we talked to everyone in that clinic. One night, they told us to put ice packs on it. The next night, we were told I should sit in a warm tub. We even tried cold laser on it. Nothing helped, and I got weaker and felt more and more defeated as the days went on. At the same time, remember, we were also dealing with Chloë having the swine flu. She was very sick too. It was definitely a low for Team Oliver.

One week after the latest surgery, I got a call from Dr. Steve. He asked me how I was doing, and I'm sure I said something like, "I'm great! Who wouldn't love an extra appendage hanging from your crotch that was so painful that I've had visions of ending it all!"

Steve stayed calm, but I could tell he felt horrible for us. He said that he wanted to take me back to the operating room to evacuate the hematoma. Hallelujah! Not that I wanted another surgery, but I could not see how this piece of baggage was going away anytime soon, and I didn't know how much longer I could handle it. This meant we were having a second surgery within a week's time. Austin and I arranged for the girls to go to Anne and Scott's house, we figured out who was going to take care of Cooper, and we headed back to the hospital.

After checking into the hospital and getting into a pre-op room, they checked my blood pressure, which was sky high. The nurse was very concerned. She asked what my pain was at.

My response was, "There isn't a number high enough."

She looked at Austin, who said, "This is serious. She never says anything higher than a five."

When we finally met with Dr. Steve that evening at the hospital, he said to us, "This can go one of three ways.

1. I will be able to make a small incision and evacuate the hematoma.
2. I will have to make a large incision, but I will still be able to evacuate the hematoma and also close that incision.
3. This would be the worst-case scenario. I will have to make a large incision, evacuate the hematoma, but I won't be able to close it."

Let's hope and pray that #3 doesn't happen.

As luck would have it, not that we believe in luck, we opened door #3! This meant that I was left with a fairly large open wound down under. Whatever.

Sometimes *whatever* was the only word that made sense. "Are you kidding me?" was a question that was way overused, so *whatever* was all I could muster. At this point, just saying goodbye to my extra appendage was a total relief!

Would the days ahead get *any* easier?

God only knows …

Chapter 24

You're Going to Put a Vacuum Where?

Have I mentioned how grateful we were for Dr. Steve? He'd made a promise that he would stick with us, and he had. Even though it had not been an easy road and unfortunate things happened, we'd always felt that we could count on him. He'd shown us many times that he truly cared. Nothing would prove it to us more than the days ahead. When you have a wound like I had, you can't just let it heal. You have to make sure that it doesn't close on the outside while leaving a pocket on the inside. If that happened, then the chance of it becoming infected was high and that would not be good. I didn't realize what we were in for immediately, which was probably a good thing, because it was now November 1. This meant that I did not have very much time before I had to get back to school.

I can remember asking Steve before I left the hospital, "How long will it take for this wound to heal?"

He responded, "We are not even going to worry about that right now."

He then went on to chat about the weather or something. Not even going to worry about it? Maybe he wasn't, but I sure as hell was! Wait a minute ... was that a good plan? I think not. Would worrying myself into a frazzle help anything? Definitely not. In Matthew 6:34 it says, "Therefore do not worry about tomorrow, for tomorrow will worry about itself. Each day has enough trouble of its own." Isn't that the truth? We were living it! In Philippians 4:6–7 it says, "Don't worry about anything; instead, pray about everything. Tell God what you need, and thank him for all he has done."

Here was my prayer: God. Yes, I'm talking to You. For some reason, I went in for surgery to repair a wound and came out of it with an even bigger wound—we're talking a gigantic one! What gives? Who in this process is not learning what they are supposed to? Remember my Oprah, little Native American healer guy, and You dream? Of course You remember. You were in it.

You said to me, "Kennedy, you are going to be okay. This is not just about you, but it's something for many people to learn from.

Who are the slow learners, God? Who is not getting what they are supposed to be getting from this? Is it me? Because, God, I think I get it! I am not in control ... You are! Your plan is perfect, and I just need to trust. My head knows it and sometimes I forget, but for the most part, I'm with You on this. It can't be Austin, can it? No way! That guy is a rock star when it comes to faith! He seems to be able to be positive no matter what, and he's really good at giving it all to You. Who are the idiots? Can we get them some tutors or something? Okay, I'm going to let it go, and I'm going to trust that You know what You are doing ... but really, God? I don't think I needed a gaping wound that goes from one hole to the ... whatever. You know what I'm talking about, and it's nasty! Can You just help me deal with the pain better? We are coming up on the third holiday season that I'm not well. Not that I'm not grateful for all that I have, because I am. I do feel blessed in this weird life, but I just want my girls to know that it's all going to be all right. Can you give them peace with everything, God? Duh, yes You can. You've got this … thankfully. At the end of the day, thank You! Thank You for the people You have put in my life and for walking through it with me … actually for carrying me, no matter what. You know I couldn't walk on my own, that's for sure!

After a couple of nights in the hospital, I was again heading home. I had now discovered that this wound that I had would need to be packed, unpacked, and repacked every day for a very long time. We are talking months, people! This would allow it to heal from the inside out. Sound fabulous? Not! How was this going to work? Well, the plan was for Austin to drive me into the clinic every day, and Dr. Steve would be the official packer. Really? So, I had to be hoisted into our truck every day, bounce my way into the clinic, which was about twenty-five minutes from our home, and then endure the packing party. All just to travel back home, lie low for twenty-four hours, and then repeat the fun. Wow, this was crazy!

We got to our Friday packing get-together, and Dr. Steve said to Austin, "Do you think you can do this on the weekend?"

Wait, what? My husband was going to be my weekend packer? Oh my goodness! Really? Was this a good plan? He actually did it and, to tell you the truth, other than it hurting like crazy, Austin did a fine job. We had been through so much together at this stage of the game, it really was okay.

I remember saying to Austin before he pulled the super long piece of blood-soaked gauze out of my vaginal wound, "This gives new meaning to the words 'in sickness and in health!'"

He looked at me and said, "I love you now more than ever, honey! You amaze me with your strength!"

By Monday morning, when we were traveling back into the clinic to meet up with our during-the-week packer, I had this feeling of depression settling in.

I asked Dr. Steve when he came into the room after we got

past the "How's it going?" question, "How long are we really going to be doing this?"

He said, "Let's see what it looks like and then we can talk about that."

He then pulled out the very long piece of nasty blood-soaked gauze and put the new one back in. When I explain it that way, it's really a good thing. Blood-soaked gauze is way better than hard-packed hematoma blood that creates a very painful pressure-filled football down under … I'm just saying.

He then said, "Why don't you get dressed and then we'll talk."

I remember saying, "No, just tell me now."

He said with reservation, "It's going to take months. The wound is not really getting any smaller. I have an idea that I want to talk to you about."

Steve went on to explain that there was something called a wound vacuum. It's used when people have very large wounds that need to heal from the inside out. He didn't think that it had ever been used on the vagina before, and he didn't know if it would work. He had already been in contact with the wound vacuum people. I didn't even know that such people existed, but they do. He said that if I was willing to try, he would set up an appointment to meet with them, and we would go from there. Was this going to be our answer to healing my wound down under?

God only knows …

Chapter 25

Trying to Enjoy Yet Another Holiday Season

The whole idea of a wound vacuum is to apply negative pressure to the wound area while sucking the fluids from the wound, increasing blood flow to the area, and allowing the wound to then heal from the inside out. That's my very non-expert definition, and putting it on my area down under was the trick. The other part that made this a special endeavor and a little nerve-wracking was that Dr. Steve was learning how to put it on, as he had never tackled this process before—on the vagina, that is. Thankfully, he was a good student. I'm not going to lie; the whole adventure was extremely painful!

Once the vacuum was on, I could see the bloody fluid come out through the tube, and I could feel the constant sucking action on my wound. I know, not fun. I remember getting home for the first time while wearing this vacuum. This meant that I had to carry the machine over my shoulder. It just looked like I was carrying a purse with a tube that was going into my pants. Nothing too out of the ordinary except that people who know me know that I'm not really a purse girl and I rarely have tubes coming out of my pants. I know, call me crazy. Seeing the fluid and hearing the sounds was what made it the freakiest—oh, and feeling it wasn't that great either.

The girls were scared at first. We really shielded them from the hematoma and all my wounds because, first of all, it scared me to see them, and secondly, they didn't need to be further scarred. We tried to be as honest as possible with them, but we didn't think they needed to see any of the blood. This made it a little difficult to explain and hard to hide because you could see the blood flowing through the tube. At first, Chloë wouldn't talk to me at all and was afraid to even come near me. Lucy, however, came and gave me a very reluctant hug.

Through tears, Lucy said, "Mom, I don't even understand what's going on. You promised us no more surgeries, and now you've just had two more. After the Clinic Faraway, we thought we were going to be done with hospitals. What is happening? Are you going to be able to go to work with this? Will you teach with this? How, Mom? You are going back to teach, right? Mom? You can hardly walk, and you can't sit at all. If you don't go back, how are we going to live? I heard you tell Anne that we could lose our insurance and our house. I hear what you and Dad say to people, Mom. You think that I don't hear you, but I do. What is going to happen to us? Why doesn't God care about us, Mom? I hate this! Why can't we be like normal people?"

When Lucy started crying, Chloë started to cry too. As you can imagine, watching my little girls cry was heartbreaking, and as it was, I was having a hard time understanding every-thing too. How was I going to explain it to them? Chloë finally spoke. She said through sobs, "Mom, I hate this too! Why can't you just be like a normal mom?"

Wow, pierce me right through the heart. She's right, God. Why? I have no words to reassure them because I'm scared too. I would like to be able to reassure them, but I can't. I just want to hold them and tell them it's going to be all right. I can't even hold my little girls because I'm in too much pain and way too weak. I can't take them upstairs to bed at night. I don't even have the energy to do anything fun with them. I feel horrible, and this is horrible! I just want to be a normal mom for even an hour! Is that too much to ask? We can't even join a support group to help us with this because nobody on the planet has ever gone through this! Are you kidding me? Who has multiple vaginal wounds that won't heal? Who puts a vacuum on it so their six- and eight-year-olds get to watch their mom's blood flow from it? No one that I know of! No one has a stomach that doesn't work! No one feels like they have the flu twenty-four seven for no reason! What on earth are brain zaps and who else has them? I'm pretty sure nobody does! Why do we have to be totally alone with this?"

This type of woe-is-me mood swing came, and thankfully, it always went. It never took me very long to get perspective. For the most part, we focused on how grateful we were and how God was working through us, but that's not to say we didn't ask why. The road we were traveling was a tough one, but just around the corner was someone fighting addiction, battling cancer, going through divorce … life is hard, people—plain and simple. Thankfully, God is good and carries us through. Without Him we would be up a creek without a paddle, or a boat for that matter—we wouldn't even have those arm floaties or a pool noodle, if you get my drift.

Eventually getting used to the wound vacuum became easier for Austin and the girls. It was not so easy for me. It had to be changed every forty-eight hours. This meant that we would travel to see Steve, or if it was the weekend, Austin got the job done. Having it on was painful, but the process of changing it was excruciating! The very scratchy, mesh-like material that was directly on the area had to be ripped out. Each time this was done, it was like ripping tape off a very raw wound. It always took some of my tissue with it. As you can imagine, this hurt like crazy!

After the first couple of times, I remember Dr. Steve saying to me, "We can go back to packing the wound if this is too painful for you."

My response was, "Do you think this is working? Is the wound getting smaller?"

He said that it was definitely working, but that he could see how horrible it was for me to go through. I reminded him that I had to be ready to go back to teaching very soon and that there was no way I was going back into a classroom of high schoolers with a bloody tube coming out of my pants or with a wound that was six inches long down under. So, let's continue with this very yucky, not much fun, extremely painful plan … if you think it's working, that is.

Dr. Steve did mention that I should probably have a plan B when it came to going back to teaching. He didn't see how I was going to be able to do it. My plan was to prove him wrong because I didn't feel like I had a choice.

Given that the holiday season was upon us and we were totally focused on my health, we bought a Christmas tree from the hardware store parking lot, barely decorated the house, and limped blindly through the days that followed. However, we were being carried by many. God put people in our lives who we didn't even know. At this point, meals were delivered to us three to four times per week by friends from church, school, and the 'hood. Our dear neighbors John and Lynn loaned us a car so that I didn't have to keep climbing into the truck. Who does that? Well, amazing people like John and Lynn, that's who. The most memorable gesture for the girls came from Patti, a friend from church. She created a version of their family's Christmas Cutdown for the girls to enjoy during the holiday season. This was made from grocery bags. It was a very long train of grocery bags stapled together to create pockets. Each pocket had a number on it and contained a gift. This meant from December 1 to December 24, Lucy and Chloë got to trade off opening a gift each day. It was a true spirit-lifter and memory that L&C will never forget!

I knew that we were never alone, I knew that You never ever left us, and I knew that all four of us were being lifted by many through this trial. Why us, God? Why are we so blessed? Why do we get to experience the very simple but profound joy of appreciation for life? Thank You! Thank You for this experience, and thank You for giving Austin and me the opportunity to teach our girls what's most important. Even though we have traveled through extreme difficulties and uncertainty, we have witnessed Your love like we never would have otherwise. You have shown us what it is like to feel lower than low but yet not be alone. You have shown us that we have courage, strength, and faith, even in times where we thought we had none. You have shown us hope when this life seemed hopeless. We are truly grateful for all of it! Yes, even for the hema-son-of-a-bitch-toma.

Will we continue to have even lower times in the future?

God only knows …

Chapter 26

Back to School After Two Years on Disability

I wore the wound vacuum for about a month and a half. It greatly reduced the wound, but did not heal it completely. This meant that I was still left with an open wound that we had to pack and unpack every day until it closed. I haven't mentioned this, but my birthday surgery didn't just give me one gift—instead I was gifted with three things. Three for the price of one! The hematoma was on the outside of the vagina, but for some reason I had also developed two significant ulcers on the inside ... bonus! I think that the hematoma pain helped me to ignore the inside pain, or maybe it was all wrapped up in one humungous pain package. Now that the outside wound was smaller and the vacuum was no longer helpful, the inside felt like I had pieces of glass constantly stabbing me from within. Oh joy! This was all happening while my back-to-school countdown was nearing fruition.

As you can imagine, this gave me immense anxiety! My back-to-school dreams turned into nightly back-to-school nightmares. The kind where I actually raced out of bed and started running. Have I mentioned that I walk in my sleep? I have done this since I was very young. Well, given that I could barely move at a snail's pace, jolting out of bed and running as fast I could did not bode well for my body's condition. In fact, Austin and I thought this just might be the reason for my non-healing ulcers, since we still had no idea why I couldn't heal. We were grasping at anything at this point.

The plan for my return to school was this: I would be dropped off at the door of the school by Austin every morning, my school friends would help me survive the day by doing all my running for me, and then Austin would pick me up at the end of the day. My niece, Marie, also gave me a love seat that I could put in the back of my classroom to use when I could no longer stand. Due to my crotch condition, sitting on anything hard was not an option, so I would have to stand all day or try to balance on one cheek while sitting. How many people do you know who teach with a crotch condition like I had? Who knows? I'm guessing it's not something that is talked about, and I'm also guessing that I was the only one! I do know for a fact that it was not easy! On top of that, my pelvic pain was so significant that while I walked, the only way that I could find comfort was to press on the left side of my pelvis. Anybody in my world who remembers this time in my life remembers that. My best friend, Marilyn, still talks about it to this day.

Many people were praying me through this time, thank goodness! Had I known the difficulty that I would face upon my return to school, I'm not sure I would have found the strength to do it. My very first day back was the beginning of the second semester, but it was a teacher in-service day. This meant that the very first time I would see the entire staff was at a morning staff meeting. I have to say, when I got to school that day, I was welcomed by everyone I saw. My friend Kathleen, who everyone calls Kat, greeted me at the door and carried my bag. Many of my school friends met me at my room and gave me a hug and reassured me that they were just a phone call away if I needed anything.

Mackenzie, the teacher in the room next to me, said, "Any time of day, I am right here. Please let me help you! I will do anything, aside from teaching math, of course."

The same could be said of almost everyone there. These people had prayed for us, fed us, given us money, given me sick days, sent us many encouraging cards and emails, had come to visit, and the list goes on. The support over the previous two years from the staff at my school was incredible! We couldn't have asked for more, that's for sure! We absolutely felt their love!

However, at that very first staff meeting, I could feel in my gut that I wasn't welcomed by everyone. It was that nagging kind of feeling that you try to push down, but it keeps creeping back up so that you can almost taste it. There was no formal "Welcome back, Kennedy!" that's for sure!

Actually, that's not entirely true. When my friend Marilyn realized that none of the people in charge were going to welcome me back, she stood up and said, "I just want to give a very warm welcome back to Kennedy! She has been gone for over two years, and we are so happy that she is here!"

Applause followed, but I still had this sense in my stomach that I wasn't completely welcome. Was this in my head? Did I do something wrong? Staring out at a group of people who fed us, gave financially to us, and supported us for two years of turmoil, how could I feel anything but love? Well, love wasn't expressed by everyone … again life is hard, not always fair, and is certainly filled with brokenness. Broken people sometimes act in unkind ways, plain and simple.

Prior to my return to school, I probably went to four or five medical appointments per week. Because of this, I knew that this was now going to have to be done after teaching all day. All my appointments were twenty to thirty minutes away from where we lived. This caused me to panic a lot! How was this going to work? Dr. Steve reassured me that he would see me after school anytime and that I didn't need to worry. My worry was not that he would fit me in after school. My worry was how would my body handle it? We would soon find out that my body couldn't handle anything very well.

My initial challenge was the overwhelming task of greeting approximately 130 students every day. Let's face it, teenagers can be tough. Try facing them while dealing with three nasty vaginal bleeding ulcers, constant nausea, and brain zaps! This really tested me, but I must say, they were awesome! I soon realized that I could still develop relationships with kids and love it! I also realized how much I'd missed my job. I loved teaching, loved teenagers, and could do math. It was a great combination!

Unfortunately, my body did not cooperate very well with this very drastic change. I made it through the days only to be taken home by Austin after school to crash into a bundle of tears, pain, and overwhelming feelings of "I can't do this!" It was extremely difficult! There were probably ten times during this third quarter of school that I would teach all day, then leave after school to race to Steve's clinic where he would try to glue, stitch, or even duct tape the ugly wounds shut. You know I'm kidding about the duct tape, right? I think it came up as a suggestion though! Anyway, as you can imagine, this became pretty close to unbearable. One day, I think in my second week back to school, the bleeding from the wound became intense. I even called Marilyn in her classroom in the middle of the day in tears.

I said to her, "I can't do this. The pain and bleeding are beating me!"

She would do and say whatever she could to encourage me, and she would always say, "You are amazing, and I love you!"

This was exactly what I needed to hear to finish the day.

Marilyn always had a way of coming up with the right words, which was why she is one of my dearest friends.

Anyway, on this day, I ran into the office after school to tell an administrator that I had to leave. This was about twenty minutes earlier than my day was supposed to end. The students were all gone at this point.

Neither of the admins were anywhere to be found, so I told Kat, the administrative assistant, "I am bleeding. I have to leave now to get to the doctor. Please let them know that I tried to find them."

She said, "Absolutely I will, and get out of here! Don't worry about things here, and please let me know if there is anything I can do for you!"

We got to Steve's clinic, where he said, "Oh my, this is really not good." He proceeded to try to stitch it together.

I remember being in so much pain during the procedure that I said, "I can't do this anymore!"

Austin always held my hand through every procedure like this with tears in his eyes. This was not only wearing on me, but on Austin and the girls too. We were all over-the-top exhausted!

Who gets their crotch stitched after working all day and gets home in time to throw up a few times, go to bed, and get up by five the next morning to repeat the process? Oh, yeah, that would be me. By the way, the stitches would never seem to hold for more than twenty-four hours. The glue, also, would never keep the wound shut. As for the duct tape, it really hurt to pull off, so it just wasn't worth it. All kidding aside, the day after the stitch-fest, during eighth hour, the last class of the day when I was usually near tears from the intense pain, I received an email from one of the administrators. The gist of it was something like this:

Kennedy,

I need to address some issues that have come up since your return to school.

You are not allowed to leave the building unless you talk to an administrator.

This is a violation of your contract and will not be tolerated. You are also not allowed to blah, blah, blah, blankety blank blah. I have been made aware of blah, blah, blah, and even more blankety blank blah.

Sincerely,
Mr. King of No Compassion

This person may as well have said, "I don't like you, you are horrible as a teacher, and I don't want anyone with your issues teaching in my building."

This person never once, since my return to school, had come to see how I was doing. Had never even entered my classroom. This person had never spoke to me directly about any concerns he had. This person was trying to create documentation of who knows what, and this person obviously didn't have one ounce of compassion in his heart. Is that too harsh? It was definitely how I felt on that day.

I was in total shock, like somebody had socked me in the gut. In my previous seventeen years of teaching, I had never received anything but praise for the job I did. I don't mean to brag too much, but I am a good teacher. That's such a funny statement, "I don't mean to brag too much, but …" When somebody clarifies a statement with, "I don't mean to, but …" it definitely means that he or she "means" to. It's like when somebody says, "I don't want to be mean but…" and we all know what's coming next is totally mean and nasty. Does that get them off the hook? No, it just tells me that they are truly mean and they know it.

Wow, that was an unexpected digression—sorry. Hey, it's my book, and I guess I can digress when I want to, and apparently, I meant to brag.

About my teaching, I'm not perfect by any means, but I know how to connect with my students, and I have developed great relationships with them. In the past from a different principal I had even received the Teacher of the Year Award. Since my return to school, I had received a message from a parent in the short time that I had been back. It was from a mom telling me how grateful she was that I was her son's teacher and that he never talked about school but was now talking about Mrs. Oliver and what a great math teacher she was. My point is, this attack on me professionally had never happened before, and given how I was feeling physically, this just about did me in. I could barely finish the class without falling apart. I called Kat immediately after school, and she came right to my room.

She read the email and just said something like, "You are amazing, and this is coming from a very small person who, for some reason, is out to get you. He doesn't want anyone that he perceives to be weak in his school. He's a total …!"

Kat could use colorful language, and she did in this situation. She is definitely someone you want on your side when times get tough!

I thought, *Why is this happening to me? I don't get this at all when there are so many people in this school who leave early almost every day and I'm sure have never told an administrator. I'm also pretty sure that they have never been written up, and they have never taught all day with a bleeding crotch and constant nausea!*

Kat also said, "I really don't know how you are doing what you are doing! The a-hole didn't know you very long before you got sick, and he only wants healthy people on his team. If it makes you feel any better, my daughters love you and always loved you as a teacher!"

Kat was very kind, but there was nothing she could really say that would help me feel like I could continue.

My reaction initially was, "I quit! I'm done! I can't keep this up, and I f-ing quit!"

Austin walked into the school that day to help me get out to the car. We both felt so defeated. He tried to encourage me, but I could tell that he also felt like we had been run over by a truck. It was one of those lowest of lows that neither of us will ever forget. It made us feel so alone and definitely brought us to our knees. And in fact, this is how we handled it. We got down on our knees. Austin did literally. He knelt next to me while I lay in bed.

His prayer was this: "Heavenly Father, we come to You feeling very defeated. It appears that Satan is working at school with Kennedy, and they just really need Your help. Please give _____ what he needs so that he can find it in his heart to do what's best for everyone. We don't know what is lacking in this person's life that he feels the need to pick on Kennedy, but please guide him, Father, in a way that only You can. Please be with Kennedy as she goes back to school tomorrow. Give her strength. Give her courage. And remind her that she is doing an incredible job! She is connecting with her students, teaching them math, but more importantly she is teaching them what it means to handle the trials of this life with grace and dignity. We love You, Father, and we know that You will see us through this like You see us through everything!"

I went back the next day with my head held high. I totally avoided Mr. King of No Compassion because that's how I roll when someone has issues with me, and I continued to teach. It might have been some of my best teaching up to that point. I made it nine weeks and then was forced to go on another medical leave. Austin and I met with the superintendent, and he couldn't have been more compassionate. He granted my leave, told us that he had been continually praying for us, and said that he would pray for my return in the fall of the next school year. He reassured us that this school district needs me, wants me, and misses me. Do I still have hope?

God only knows ...

Chapter 27

Spring 2010: Two More Surgeries, Really?

Since 2007, I've had eight surgeries all on my area down under, too many office procedures to count, at least twenty getaways to the Clinic Faraway, over umpteen mega zillion miles to medical appointments and hospitals, and yet the only diagnosis I'd received was gastroparesis with a very large hiatal hernia. I'd seen "eating disorder" written in my chart, been asked if I'm depressed hundreds of times, have told the story just under a million times, and yet I still have hope. When Dr. Steve said, "I think I can fix this" two more times over the next five months, Austin and I agreed to go back to the operating room. We didn't know for sure that the surgeries would be successful, but we knew that if there was a chance that the situation could improve, then it was worth it for us to take that chance. We knew that living like we were living was not an option if there was some hope that it could change.

This became a situation where we had to make the best decision for us with the information that we had. Did we receive criticism from people? Absolutely. Were we questioned about the decision to have another surgery? Yes, but nobody knew the road we were traveling. Nobody could truly put themselves in our shoes. We had to trust, keep the faith, and not look back. When surgeries number nine and ten failed, we felt, again, like we were so alone. We questioned God's purpose and questioned ourselves and our decisions.

We had one appointment with Dr. Brown, who was the surgeon who'd assisted Dr. Steve in surgery number ten. She was also the GYN surgeon who performed surgeries two through four.

Dr. Brown told us at the appointment, "Dr. Hopkinson and I are done with you. You need to consider total vaginal reconstruction. Good luck."

We left from yet one more appointment where we felt like we were being shoved to the wayside. We learned later that even though Dr. Brown had presumed to speak for Dr. Steve, he did not feel that way and continued to keep his promise not to ditch us.

I can remember saying to Austin, "These doctors are just people. They have been given special gifts, but they, too, are not in control. I want to believe that God still has a plan, and if I remember back to my dream two years ago, then I have to hang on to that promise and believe that everything is going to be okay."

I then had to get ready to go back to school that fall. This was 2010, and my first surgery was in 2007! I'm only repeating that information because, oh my goodness! Are you kidding me? My first symptoms began in 2005. Just to give you the time perspective here. For five years we had been suffering on this unknown, crazy, out-of-control journey!

I still had three vaginal ulcers, and I struggled with my digestive system and had to take medication to eat, which didn't always work. I continued to feel lousy most of the time. What kept me going? My girls, my husband, and a faith that remained strong. I needed to accept the fact that this was maybe going to be who I was for the rest of my life. Maybe I was always going to feel like this. Maybe things were never going to improve. Could I still find somebody who was suffering more than I was? For sure. I knew that I didn't have to look very far to find someone who was in worse shape than I was. Did this mean that my trials weren't important? No, but it helped give me perspective, and it helped me to think outside of myself, which in turn helped with my mental health. Does that make sense? Ultimately, if everyone put their lives up for grabs and I got to choose anyone else's life to live, I knew that I would take mine. For sure, without a doubt, I would not trade my life for anything. I still felt blessed and grateful for all that I had, no question.

What actually amazes me the most at this very moment while I'm writing is that I just glossed over two failed surgeries. Two of ten! Some people have never gone through one surgery, let alone several very horrible, painful ones on their areas down under! All I can say is wow.

Would there be any more surgeries in my future?

God only knows …

Chapter 28

Dr. Thomas Kennedy

Throughout this journey, I have talked about many people. Dr. Stephen Hopkinson was one doctor who became our advocate, expert, and friend. He was invaluable to us! Another person, who I have not mentioned on this unpaved, full-of-potholes road yet is Dr. Thomas Kennedy. He is someone, like Steve, who we believe was an angel sent from God. Austin had known Dr. Kennedy as his chiropractor since the 1990s. I started going to see him when I was pregnant with Chloë in 2002.

Isn't it crazy that his name is Dr. Kennedy? It's almost as if we were meant to cross paths because my name is Kennedy. Oh wait, I forgot, all names in this book have been changed. It's not fate at all. It's just my clever thinking while writing this. I do like the name though.

Dr. Kennedy or Dr. Tom, as we like to call him, was not only an amazing chiropractor, but he was also a very gifted nutritional expert, environmental expert, and the most gifted healer that we knew. He could figure out things that many of the other doctors that we were seeing could not. My explanation of what Tom does cannot possibly do it justice, so I am not even going to try.

During our journey, we would sometimes go to see Tom up to three times a week. He was absolutely the one person who kept us going. He not only treated me, but he treated all four of us many, many times! We would consult with Tom on almost everything that we did, and although Tom doesn't support surgery as being the answer, we never felt judged by him for the decisions that we made. We gave total credit to Tom for using his God-given gifts to keep us moving forward in a semi-upright fashion.

Tom would meet us at his office anytime we called him. He even took our phone calls late at night while we were at the Clinic Faraway in another state. To say that we would trust Tom with our lives is putting it lightly. Furthermore, we weren't the only patients that he saw. His appointment schedule was always booked, and it never ceased to amaze me how he always greeted us with a smile and a kind word even after being on his feet treating others the entire day.

Dr. Tom would often talk about our situation being one that kept him up at night. Unfortunately, for him, he lost a lot of sleep! He was continually researching ways that he could help us. He desperately wanted to figure out why I wasn't healing and why I had the debilitating GI issues. I'm pretty sure Tom spent more hours helping us than all the other doctors combined. Because of that, he held a very special place in our hearts and always will.

Chloë said one time, "Even a thousand chocolate sheet cakes couldn't be enough to show our thanks to Dr. Tom!"

Would he eventually be the one to figure out what was going on?

God only knows …

Chapter 29

Politics, a Trip to Another Clinic Faraway, and Lice

How would I go back to work full-time after two failed surgeries with three bleeding ulcers, a stomach that still didn't work all the time, an unsupportive administrator, and absolute exhaustion? I really had no idea. I guessed just by taking it one day at a time, sometimes one hour at a time. It kind of all seems like a blur to me now, and except by the grace of God, I don't know how I did it. I would see Dr. Tom and Dr. Steve regularly because I seemed to get a lot of infections and still felt like garbage pretty much twenty-four seven. I also tried acupuncture, Healing Touch, and other alternative forms of medicine. I was willing to try just about anything, hoping there was something out there that would kick this situation to the curb. Unfortunately, it never happened.

My routine was to be dropped off at the door of the high school every day, get through a day of teaching, be picked up by Austin, go home, and head right to bed. I recall being contacted by Lucy's fourth-grade teacher one month into the school year because she was concerned that Lucy was totally exhausted. I remember thinking, *I know—we all are. We are all walking zombies!*

Just because I was the one with the visible wounds if you looked down under didn't mean that Austin and the girls weren't struggling too. All four of us were suffering. Was it because of the stress? Was it because of everything we had gone through over the last six years? We really didn't know.

We took Lucy to the doctor and explained to her pediatrician that we'd gotten this call from her teacher and just wanted to check it out. Appearance-wise, Lucy had very dark circles under her eyes. This wasn't new, but I guess we had gotten used to it. Her doctor was concerned enough to run some tests. She didn't think that anything would come of it, but she decided to x-ray Lucy's sinuses just to make sure they were clear. Well, it turned out Lucy had a very significant sinus infection. Huh? Lucy had these frequently, but usually there were some symptoms. We got her on an antibiotic. Then we were sent to a pediatric sinus specialist to see if there was something else we could do because she had these so frequently. I remember none of this doctoring really helped. Lucy continued to be extremely exhausted and continued to have frequent sinus issues.

That school year was exhausting for everybody. I don't really want to get into politics, but the political firestorm in Wisconsin contributed to the isolation that Austin and I already felt because of my illness. This would be the year that the governor of our state and the Republican party would attack our educational system. Prior to this, I had no idea how many people in our state felt such total resentment toward teachers. People didn't believe we should get paid for what we do or receive the benefits that we do. I had close friends tell me that they were on the other side. They felt teachers were way overpaid. Huh? This tore apart families, damaged many relationships, and just added so much negative energy to an already uphill battle. Given the way that I was feeling physically, this took a major toll on my health and added a ton of stress.

As I continued to doctor throughout this school year, Dr. Steve continued to investigate where he could send me to get another opinion. He researched experts in our area and in states around us. Ultimately, he found a gynecological expert in Michigan. He got us an appointment over my spring break. So, instead of having the week to recoup from the utter exhaustion, and instead of traveling to a warm destination like so many people get to do on spring break, we planned a six-hour road trip to the new Clinic Faraway. We arranged for the girls to stay with my sister and off we went. Woohoo, spring break at a new doctor's office … yuck!

It was so nerve-wracking meeting new doctors and going through the entire story, but if it meant we could get help, then we were willing to do it. I recall when Dr. Eaves came into the room that my gut told me, *Oh no. I can sense it already. She's not going to be nice.*

I could always call it immediately, and I was correct again. Dr. Eaves spoke in a demeaning and very cold manner. She was definitely not the warm fuzzy that I had hoped for.

As we neared the exam part of the appointment, I was a shaking rash from head to toe. As Dr. Eaves did the zillionth pelvic exam of my life, Austin and I could tell right away that she was alarmed by the condition of my area down under, and she actually did have compassion. She told us that she wanted to have two other doctors come in, but it would mean that we would have to wait for them to be free. It was quite amazing, but all of a sudden, all three doctors became available. That kind of immediate doctor availability never happens! This just tells you how nasty my down under situation was.

All three doctors were very concerned that the ulcers on the inside were getting deep enough that they might form a hole between the vaginal and the anal wall. They did some very painful testing and ultimately came up with nothing more than Steve had. The ulcers were nasty, and the hole wasn't there quite yet, but the wall was very thin. They thought that it would become a hole at some point without a serious intervention. They all agreed that it was a mess, looked very painful, and they didn't know why. So, we drove all the way to another Clinic Faraway and really didn't get any new solutions. I remember calling Steve from our hotel before our journey home. I could hear it in his voice—the hope he'd had for the appointment was definitely gone. It felt very depressing.

On top of it all, you are not going to believe what adventure we got to experience next. Lice came to live with us! This just about sent us to the funny farm. It was a Sunday night before a long week of school ahead. Chloë started complaining about her head itching. You know when someone says that, everyone starts to immediately itch. I'm sure you are itching right now as you read this. Sorry.

Unfortunately, there was a reason that her head itched. Those very blucky yucky bugs had not only made a home on her head but on mine too! Are you kidding me? I was a total freak! Austin and I stayed up for an entire night cleaning, bagging all our stuff, and treating our heads. I went to school at four in the morning to make sub plans. I remember going to the restroom at school while I was working and realized I also had blood everywhere down under from my ulcers.

In that school bathroom, I sobbed and prayed, "You have got to be kidding me! This life is kicking my butt big time! I can't deal with bugs too! Aghhhhhhhhhhhhhhhhhh! Please, God, stop all of it! We need it to end now! Bleeding ulcers, throwing up, umpteen surgeries, people who hate teachers, and now bleeping lice! What gives?"

I got home around five that morning. We tried to go to bed but couldn't sleep. My body was nearing total collapse. How was I going to keep going? The school year was several weeks from being done, but I still felt like I was going to die on most days. How had I made it this far? At this point, we were just praying that I survived until the end of the school year. God gave me the strength to do what I needed to do, which was totally amazing when I look back on it. Through the crazy stress, the unbelievable pain, and the constant flulike symptoms I kept moving forward and teaching kids. How?

God only knows ...

Chapter 30

Austin Gets Sick

The school year finished, and I had survived! I really don't know how, but that doesn't matter. What matters is, I did it! It was like I had finished a mega-marathon or something. When Austin picked me up on that last day, I got in the car and we just stared at each other.

He said, "Well, honey, you made it! I have no idea how you did it every day with how you are feeling, but you did. I think all four of us deserve a break and a summer of total rest."

He said a prayer right there in front of the high school, "Thank You, Father, for giving Kennedy the strength to survive the school year. We know she couldn't have done it without You and without the awesome people we have in our lives. We continue to ask for healing for her. Please, Father, heal her! All our trust is in You. Amen."

Let the summer begin!

One thing that we enjoyed doing as a family to get away from our stressful life was camping. You might be thinking, *what?* Especially if you are not a camper, but our type of camping was not really roughing it. I like the type where you have air conditioning, your own bathroom, and a refrigerator. I know, not really camping, but whatever. It was a way for us to escape the madness rather inexpensively, if only for a night or two. We loved to pack up our camper and head out. We wouldn't go far. Usually just an hour from home, but Lucy and Chloë loved it and so did Austin and I. One of our favorite destinations was to a campground just an hour north of our house.

On this occasion, it was a Saturday night and our plan was to leave the next day. We got everything ready to go. Both girls had friends over the night before we left. Chloë and her friend camped out in our great room, and Lucy and her friend camped out upstairs in our loft area. I remember feeling absolutely wiped out and regretting our decision to let them have people over, but we were always trying to let them do normal things even though I felt like garbage.

We finally got everyone to bed and then Austin and I went to bed. Nothing seemed out of the ordinary until about midnight when I realized Austin was not in bed. I lay there thinking about what was left to do before leaving the next day.

The next thing I knew, Austin walked into the bedroom and told me that he had been throwing up. He said he felt horrible. "Oh no!" was all I could say. I asked him if he thought it was something he ate or the stomach flu or what? It was kind of dumb because I know that when this is me throwing up in the middle of the night, which it usually is, the last thing I want to do is answer a bunch of questions about why. I was right about that because he just wanted me to shut up and of course didn't have any of the answers to my questions.

I lay there thinking about everything. My mind was a little crazy. I find that I do my most outrageous thinking in the middle of the night. Can you relate? I can go from one subject to the next and back again within seconds. I can get my heart racing a million miles an hour, no problem. I have a strong faith, but that doesn't mean I always remain calm.

I started to try to focus on our blessings to still my racing heart. I thought about how I made it through the school year and hadn't lost my job for health reasons. I thought about how I was still here, and I hadn't died yet. I focused on the fact that the girls were doing okay. They still struggled big time in school, but they were kind, happy, and well-rounded kids. They often showed us what it meant to truly have faith!

Austin had been totally healthy, as far as we knew … well, shit! What if he's not? What if this is more than just the flu? Life with both of us sick would be a nightmare, to say the least. I should be thankful that it has just been me. I kept telling myself, *It's just a stomach bug or the flu. It will be all better in twenty-four hours.*

I then said a prayer, "God, it's me again. Thanks for keeping us together moving forward. Thanks for getting us through an entire school year despite the bleeding ulcers, the nausea, the political firestorm, the failed trip to the other Clinic Faraway, and yes, thank You for helping us survive the lice. I just have one request tonight, Lord. Can You make Austin's illness be just a twenty-four-hour deal? Please? Thanks, God, for everything and a whole lot more. Oh, and God? Could You make my mind stop and let me sleep? Please?"

Would He answer all my prayers?

God only knows …

Chapter 31

It's Not the Stomach Flu

The next morning, Austin was still not feeling well but said that we should still go camping. He had called the campground and was told that we couldn't get our money back if we cancelled our reservation. Knowing Austin, this was what really made him determined to go camping. Given that we were only going an hour away, he decided that he would be okay, and he really wanted to get away for a couple of nights. The girls and I did the last-minute packing, and we headed out. It was a gorgeous summer day, and setting up camp wasn't too difficult as it was something we had done so many times. We happened to get a pull-through campsite, which made setting up even easier. It was obvious, however, that Austin was not feeling well. Lucy and Chloë went right to the pool when we got there, and eventually Austin and I made our way there.

Given that I had these nasty bleeding ulcers, going into chlorinated water would not feel very good, so I just laid on a deck chair and watched the girls swim. Austin usually got in with them, but he was moving pretty slowly himself and just sat by the edge. I remember watching another family where everyone was in the water having a great time. I felt the pain of what this chronic situation had robbed from our family, and it brought tears to my eyes. Our girls really didn't know what it was like to have all four of us enjoying a fun activity like this all together. Little did I know that it was just about to get a million times worse.

Austin had a sleepless night, which meant I did too. By morning he agreed that he should go to urgent care or something. This told me how bad he really was feeling because getting him to go to the doctor was like getting Chloë to sleep through the night as a toddler—nearly impossible! Austin told me that I should stay at the campsite with the girls so that they could go swimming and not be stuck at a doctor's office. He drove to the urgent care in the town we were in.

After he got there and saw someone, they immediately told him that he needed to go to the hospital. He called me and told me this. I instantly felt a nervous chill throughout my body. I asked him a lot of questions and soon realized that he had no answers. Ironically, my sister happened to be on her way there to meet my niece, Elisa. Elisa lived an hour north, so this was a good meeting place for them. I called Anne and asked if she could come get the girls and then drop me off to be with Austin. Of course she was happy to do that. Elisa got to our campsite first.

Right away she said to me, "What is going on?"

I told her about his recent illness, but she could tell how worried I was. She said to me, "You guys cannot catch a break! I don't know how you do it! Let's just hope that it's nothing serious."

Lucy and Chloë were so excited to see Elisa and her little girl, Rose, that they were preoccupied. I didn't think that they understood what was going on, but as my sister Anne pulled into the campground, Lucy came running up to me.

She said, "Mom, is Dad going to be okay? What is wrong

with him, Mom? Why does he have to go to the doctor? Is it something bad, Mom? Are you okay, Mom? What is going on?"

Chloë then came over and hugged me and said, "I am going with you!"

I tried to reassure them that it was going to be okay and that they were going to have fun with Anne, Elisa, and Rose. We also had our dog, Cooper, with us, so we just had to put him in our camper while we went to meet Austin at the urgent care.

After they dropped me off at the clinic, Austin and I then drove to a town not far from where we were where they had a small hospital. Austin was moaning and groaning all the way there, and he was driving! Wouldn't you think he would let me drive? Stubborn man! I was thinking, *Gallbladder, appendix, kidney stones? What could it be?*

I said a prayer to myself, *Please, God. I'm not sure how much more we can take here. Austin is our rock, so please … just please take his pain and make this something simple like constipation or a kidney stone. I'm begging for You to ease his pain with a simple and not scary fix. Okay, God?*

After we got to the hospital, they took us back into a room and asked Austin all kinds of questions. They had him pee into a cup, and they did some blood work. Then they said they wanted to take a picture of his abdomen. I prayed the entire time that he was gone. When they wheeled him back into the room, the doctor explained to us what was going on. He said that Austin had what appeared to be air in his abdominal cavity. They now needed to do a CT scan. They took Austin while I waited. I started calling people.

I called my mom, my brother Jack, and my sister Anne. I said to Anne, "You are not going to believe this. It's not good. They just took him for a CT scan. I don't know what is going on. Why is this happening? I don't think it's going to be good news. Are you kidding me? We can't do this!"

Anne said to me, "Kennedy, you have to stay calm. Romans 8:28, Ken. You don't even know anything yet. Don't borrow trouble. You can do this. Be strong!"

"They are coming back, I have to go!"

The doctor told us that Austin's colon was perforated. Wait, what? What does that even mean? Austin had a colonoscopy within the last year and everything had looked good. How does this even happen out of the blue without warning? I explained to the doctor that we needed to get Austin to a bigger hospital closer to where we lived.

The doctor told me, "Absolutely not, Mrs. Oliver."

He then told me that Austin wasn't going anywhere for a while. He said that it could be weeks. He said that he would eventually need surgery, and that hopefully it would heal enough to have a surgery that would not be an emergency. What was he telling us? I couldn't even wrap my head around what was happening. He said that Austin was very, very sick.

"Really, God? Why don't You answer any of our prayers? I asked You to ease his pain with an easy fix. Seriously ... surgery? Are you kidding me? What the hell? Why was this happening?"

God only knows ...

Chapter 32

What Did This Even Mean?

I remember trying to wrap my head around what was happening. I said to the doctor, "You don't understand what we have been through. We need to get to a bigger hospital! We don't live close, and our doctors are not here in this town. How can we get Austin to a bigger hospital?"

He very calmly said to me, "You don't understand, Mrs. Oliver. This is very serious. We need to get him on an IV antibiotic immediately. He will be staying in this hospital indefinitely."

Huh? Indefinitely? What the hell does that even mean? I felt so confused and overwhelmed. Austin, on the other hand, was very calm ... of course he was. The doctor left us alone, and Austin looked at me with a smile on his face. Who can smile at a time like this? Only Austin Oliver, that's who!

He said, "Life is never dull, that's for sure. You are going to have to figure out how to get the camper and take it home. Please make sure that you hook it up to the truck correctly and blah, blah, blah ..."

Seriously? Me? I was going to have to get the camper home? I don't even drive the truck. I don't hook up campers. I haven't even driven myself much in the last four years. I can't even lift anything without feeling like my insides are going to fall out onto the floor. My bleeding ulcers are not going to like this! How is this going to work? God? What the fuck?

I left Austin for a minute since I felt like I might throw up right on him. I couldn't even breathe. My heart was racing, and I started to shake.

The guy behind the desk came up to me and said, "Are you okay? Can I help you?"

I said to him while trying to catch my breath, "Can you hook up a camper, pack up all our stuff, and get it back home for us?"

He stared at me blankly.

After what seemed like a long stare down, I said, "I don't even know what I'm saying, but I do need help. My husband is going to be here indefinitely. I have two little girls, a dog, and a camper up at the campground, and I have three bleeding ulcers down under. Do you need to know any of that? Of course you don't, but I don't know what I'm going to do."

With sympathy in his eyes, he said to me, "Can I call someone for you?"

"Yes, you can. Wait, no … I can. I can do this and I will. Thank you for caring."

I got on the phone. I called my brother Jack first. He answered, and I didn't even have words.

He said, "Ken, are you there?"

Through tears I said, "This can't be happening. He's here for a while. He's really sick … oh God, he's really, really sick! Jack, I can't lose him! Oh my goodness, what if I lose him?" I then began to cry.

"Ken, Diane and I are on our way. Don't worry about the camper. I will take care of it. We will be there in an hour." Diane is my sister-in-law, Jack's wife.

I then called Dr. Tom. I explained to him what was going on with Austin. He first said that yes, we needed to stay there.

He reassured me that this was what was best for Austin right now. I re-explained what the doctor had already told me. He told me what a perforated colon could do and how very serious it was. He explained how the contents of Austin's colon would be leaking into his body. He said that this was extremely toxic, and it was important for that hole to close for Austin to get better. Tom's reassurance was just what I needed to hear. He told me to call him and keep him updated, and he said that he would be praying for us.

I then called Rae, our oldest daughter, who lived two hours away. I also called Austin's mom, and my sister Anne. I told Anne to please stay calm for Lucy and Chloë and to give them a hug from us. Kind of funny, me asking someone else to stay calm? Are you f-ing kidding me? I asked her to bring them to the hospital, but to wait until we were in a room. As I said it, I fell apart. In a room? A hospital room for Austin? This was not supposed to be happening. Austin was our rock. He took care of us. I stay in hospital rooms … Austin does not! What were we going to do? The girls were going to have to rely on me? I certainly have not received any supermom awards … I would have received the award for "the mom who can hardly do a damn thing" if there was such an award! I can barely take care of myself. I can't even … God? What are You thinking? How long are we going to be here?

God only knows …

Chapter 33

Austin's Long Health Journey Has Begun

Jack and Diane took care of the camper. Anne brought the girls to the hospital, my mom and my sisters Lee and Joy came there too, and my brother-in-law Scott drove up to get Cooper. Austin was put on morphine right away. He had one of those buttons where he could administer his own pain meds when he needed them. He pushed the button constantly. I could tell the girls were nervous when they got to the hospital. They had come to visit me on many occasions in the hospital, and now they were visiting their daddy. It all felt so terribly wrong. It was a nightmare.

We decided that the girls wouldn't stay very long and that they would go back to our home with my family. They were both on the verge of tears when they said goodbye to their daddy. I think they were also in shock. Who wasn't? I walked them out into the hall and promised them that I would be home later. I was the one who was in tears. As I watched them walk down the hall, they looked so little. All of a sudden, Lucy turned around and came running back to me. She hugged me and then started singing. It was the absolute sweetest moment. What she sang was the chorus from the Bob Marley song "Three Little Birds."

"Don't you worry, about a thing. Cuz every little thing, is gonna be all right. I love you, Mom!"

Oh my goodness, my ten-year-old had more faith than I did and was the one who was taking care of me.

I remember driving home from the hospital that night with my sister Joy. What kind of crazy world was I in? I left my very sick husband in a hospital almost an hour away from home. It was a horrible feeling. When we got home, I recall pulling up to our house and seeing several of my family and friends taking care of everything. They were helping to get our camper back into our garage among other things. There was also a stream of water flowing from our garage. My brother-in-law was walking out of the garage shaking his head.

As I got closer I asked, "What's going on?"

He said, "Apparently your freezer got turned off while you were gone and it's defrosted."

Really? I get to deal with a freezer full of thawed food? Was this a joke? What comedian thought this was a funny addition to my already very sucky, no good, very bad day?

At this point, my family had decided that the girls and I needed company. They told me that one of them would stay with us every night while Austin was in the hospital.

I said to them, "That could be weeks! You guys don't have to do that. We don't even have an extra bed."

My sister Joy said that it was the least they could do. They wanted the girls and me to feel safe and taken care of. They didn't want us to be alone and knew that this would be an easy way that they could help. The girls and I were so grateful! Thankfully, I have a big family, and they were all willing to take a turn! This made a huge difference for both Lucy and Chloë and for me!

As I got ready for bed that night, the phone rang. It was Austin. He wanted to talk to the girls. I told him they were both in bed, and just as I said it two heads called down to me from upstairs.

"We are up, Mom! We want to talk to Dad!"

They came running down the stairs. As Lucy talked on the phone, she was fighting back tears.

The last thing she said to him was, "Sweet dreams, hugs and kisses, God bless you! I love you!"

This was always the last thing we said to the girls every night. Chloë then got on the phone, and she started to cry.

She said, "When are you coming home? I want you to come home now."

And then you could just hear her agreeing to everything he was saying. I'm sure he was telling her to be strong, to be a big helper, and to remember that God was taking care of us, so don't worry.

We decided that night the girls would sleep with me in our room. This was a comfort to me and to them. How long would Austin be in the hospital?

God only knows …

Chapter 34

Our New Life

The next morning, I got up around five after only sleeping maybe an hour. I walked around the house like a zombie. I then went out to the camper to see what I needed to do to get it cleaned up. I opened the door and just stared at all our stuff. Unfortunately, when you go camping, you take a lot of stuff even if it's only for a couple of days. The girls' bikes were right in the doorway, as was the cooler, the pool noodles, our grill, a couple of bins of who knows what. It all needed to be taken out to even get in the door.

I started to lift stuff and realized, *What the hell am I doing?*

I could feel the ulcers in my crotch start to throb. If I tried to lift anything, it felt like my insides were going to come crashing to the floor. There was this pressure like a woman has when she's about to have a baby and knows there is no way that she can hold it in.

I thought, *It would be bad if I start doing this camper clean-up and all my organs that are supposed to stay on the inside of my body end up on our garage floor. I'm not sure our family can handle much more right now, so maybe I better just shut the door and go back inside the house.*

So that's what I did. I just walked away.

As I got inside, the phone was ringing. It was Austin.

"Hi, honey. How was your night?" he said.

I knew that I had to be strong so that he wouldn't worry about anything.

I said to him, "The girls and I all camped out in our room. They are still sleeping, and I'm just wandering around here in a fog. How are you feeling?"

He wasn't very positive, which is unlike Austin. He said the pain was intense, and he was glad he had the morphine button. He told me I didn't need to come there. He said I should just stay home and relax.

Huh? Was he kidding? First of all, is that what he would do if I was in the hospital? Absolutely not! I'm sure he was trying to ease my burden of figuring it all out, but it just made me feel like he didn't need me. I told him that I would be coming as soon as I got ready and that he couldn't do anything about it.

That is what I did. I got ready, dropped the girls off at my sister's house, and headed to the hospital. My mom wanted to come with me, but I just wanted to go alone. It was crazy driving up there. For the last several years, I had hardly driven anywhere by myself, and even as a passenger, I'd had several pillows that I used to make riding in a car bearable. And now, here I was driving forty-five minutes away, sitting on my nasty ulcerated crotch, on a road that I swear is the bumpiest road on the planet to see my very sick husband. This life totally sucked, and I didn't see it getting better anytime soon.

Not much changed for Austin in those first couple of days at the hospital. He was not allowed to put anything into his mouth. He couldn't even have a drop of water. His colon needed to heal, and the only way that it could would be if nothing passed through it. It felt like torture to watch, and I knew it was worse than torture for him to go through. As I was getting ready to say goodbye to him on his third night there, he grabbed my hand and told me that he had something to say to me.

He said very slowly and through lots of pausing and gasping breaths, "Honey, you know that I love you and the girls very much, but I think it's time for me to go. I've been praying for God to just take me. I have made peace with Him, and I'm ready. I know that it will be hard, but you can do it. You are very strong! Please know how much I love you! You have made me the happiest man in the world."

I thought I might explode on him as I said, "What the hell are you saying? You are giving up? Not happening, dude! Do you think I have fought like crazy to survive my own health nightmare to let you just say after only three days, 'I'm good to go!' I don't think so, buddy! You fight, and you fight hard! Dying is not an option, so get it out of your head right now! The girls and I deserve to have you fight for your life, so you better dig deep and ask God for strength!"

He started to speak, "I'm just ..."

I interrupted, of course, "You are just going to have to get tough and fight through this! I am not listening to this anymore! I love you, I need you, and we are going to survive this no matter how long it takes, so don't think you get to quit on me that easy. You are strong, and this is not your time! Do you hear me? You do not get to choose this! Actually, I'm pretty sure God gets to ... so stop this crazy talk right now!"

He looked at me with a slight smirk. "Wow, you are hardcore. I guess I will keep fighting. I hope you know how much I love you!"

I couldn't believe that conversation had just happened. Are you kidding me? After all we'd gone through, he thought he could just bail? I think not! Our life was totally out of control! God? Help us please ... now! We can't do this on our own, and we need some serious intervention!

I drove home that night sobbing all the way. I remember that I was bleeding right through my shorts. What was happening? I went straight to Anne and Scott's house hoping that the girls would be there. I needed them. We needed to be together. When I got there, I walked in and it was very quiet. Anne, Scott, and my niece Jenny were out on their back deck and the girls weren't there. They came through the house to greet me. Anne took one look at me and she knew.

"Ken, what's going on? Are you okay? You are not okay. Oh Ken."

I tried to talk, but couldn't. They just came and hugged me, and Jenny, who has special needs and can be very emotional, started to wail. Scott had to take her outside. She and Austin had a very special connection, so this was very hard for Jenny.

I couldn't even speak, but I did get out that I needed Lucy and Chloë. They were with my niece Marie. Anne called her and asked her to bring them home. I got in the van and went home. Our house was empty except for Cooper. He seemed shocked too. Marie then pulled up with the girls. They came running in, and we just hugged for the longest time. They didn't even ask about Austin.

Lucy just kept saying as if to reassure all of us, "Dad is okay. He's going to be okay. Right, Mom? He's okay. He's going to be okay. Right? Mom … he is going to be okay!"

Chloë just kept hugging me tighter and tighter.

Marie said, "Let's pray. Dear God, the Olivers need You right now. We need to know that You are watching over Austin and that he is going to be okay. Our hope is in You, Jesus. Please heal Lucy and Chloë's daddy. Amen."

Was Austin truly going to be okay?

God only knows …

Chapter 35

Now It's an Emergency

The morning of June 29, 2011, started with a phone call from Austin. He was feeling a little better, which was such a blessing. He was excited because his doctors thought the perforation was healing, so they were going to let him try some apple juice. I felt like God was answering our prayers. This was a huge relief!

So when I got out of the shower to a phone call saying that he had taken a turn for the worse, I was shocked and in disbelief! How could this be happening? He'd told me himself that he thought he was turning a corner. Is this really true? What planet was I on? This couldn't be happening!

Austin's temperature had skyrocketed, and his pain level went through the roof. After the nurse's phone call, I could hardly think. I knew that I needed to hurry, and yet it felt like my feet were stuck in quicksand. I wanted to get out of the house before Lucy and Chloë got back from swim practice. I couldn't face them with this news, so I asked my sister Anne if she could get them. Each step forward was harder and harder to take. This road we were traveling felt insane!

Before leaving the house, I sent a text to my friends Becky and Cheri. If anybody had a direct line to God, it was these two. Unfortunately, Cheri never got my text, but Becky called me right away. I was driving, at this point, like a mad woman.

I just kept yelling to her, "You have to pray now! I can't lose him! What if I lose him? God wouldn't do that to us, would He? This is a nightmare! He is very sick and will need emergency surgery today. Please pray now!"

We then got cut off because I was driving in the valley.

By the time I got to the hospital, I'd screamed myself hoarse. I went from swearing to crying to pleading and back again multiple times on my forty-five-minute drive. When I got to Austin's floor, I passed the nurse's station where Austin's nurse, Sharon, was sitting. She told me that his temp was 103.6 and that he was in a lot of pain. They were struggling to keep him comfortable. She said that we had some decisions to make. Were we going to do the surgery there, or did we want him transported to a bigger hospital? It was a difficult decision because I didn't want Austin to have to endure the transport, but the surgeon who would do the surgery there was leaving on vacation the next day. Ultimately, we decided that we needed to get to the bigger hospital.

Unfortunately, there weren't any beds available at the moment. I couldn't wrap my head around that. No vacancy in the entire hospital? No vacancy is a thing when it comes to hospitals? Really? I couldn't believe that could be true, but it was. Well, of course … you only have a certain number, but really? Now? Thankfully, we didn't have to wait too long. While we were waiting, several of our people came to be with us. Becky, to whom I'd been screaming on the phone with, dropped everything she had planned to do with two of her adult sons, Ryan and Tyler, and they all came right away. My mom and my sister Lee came. Because our pastor was out of town, another pastor from our town also traveled with his wife to the hospital to be with us.

As we were waiting, Tyler and Becky came and prayed with us. This was something that gave us an incredible sense of peace. Tyler prayed for Zorro, which is what some of our friends call Austin because of a game of Catch Phrase that we played at a Christian Bible camp that we love to go to. This brought a smile to Austin's face, which we hadn't seen much of lately. He also prayed for the doctors, the nurses, and for the girls who were anxiously waiting for news. They were still with my sister Anne.

As it came time to get Austin ready for the ambulance transport, Austin and I had some time together. We talked about the journey we had been on. Who knew back on July 24, 1999, our wedding day, where this life would take us? We did mention that a vacation from it all in the future would be nice. As I was helping Austin get dressed for the trip, there was this sense of irony. For the past several years, this had been Austin's role with me. He'd dressed me on many occasions, packed my wounds, and administered my meds. He prayed for my health and my strength and for me to feel a sense of His peace. How would I do in my new role?

God only knows …

Chapter 36

Surgery for Austin

After saying goodbye to Austin, I got in the van with Becky and we followed the ambulance. It was such a surreal drive. I still couldn't believe that it was even happening. I remember calling Dr. Tom's office before we passed by asking everyone there to pray for us. I also got a phone call from our daughter Rae saying that she would meet us at the hospital. At the small hospital we were at, they explained to us that Austin would have part of his colon removed and that they would probably have to give him an ostomy to allow his body to heal. An ostomy? What was that? In my layman's terms, it's a new hole that is created that would come out of Austin's abdominal area and would allow the solid waste to come out. Yeah, Austin would have poop coming out of that hole into a bag that would be attached by adhesive. Huh? We would have to have training on that new apparatus for sure!

This was not even a concern, however, at this point. Who cared about that when my husband was fighting for his life? When we got to the hospital, they got us into a pre-op-type room. We eventually met with a team of doctors that would be in the operating room for Austin's surgery. The surgery wouldn't even happen until later in the evening. This was an extremely long day! Can anyone say exhausting?

As Austin and I waited in the pre-op room right before they were going to take him back to surgery, he was talking about how awful the ambulance ride was. He said every bump felt like he was going to die. This was very upsetting to me because, first of all, Austin rarely complains. Secondly, they reassured me that they would give him enough medication that he would feel no pain. Grrrrrrrrrrrrr!

When the nurse came to get him, they told me that I could walk along and hold his hand. I did that until they said we had to say goodbye.

I leaned down and said a simple prayer with him. "God. Yes, I'm talking to You. This is not Austin's time to join You. Do you hear me? Keep him safe, and bring him out of this! Amen!"

I told him that I loved him and that making peace with God was not an option, so he'd better get that out of his head! I then watched him being wheeled away, and I broke down and sobbed.

A nurse came up to me and said, "Kennedy? You have a friend here."

Well, hallelujah, because I really needed a friend at this stage of the game.

She took me through some doors where I was greeted by Marcia, a dear friend from church, who was also a nurse at the hospital. She took one look at me and gave me a big hug. She reassured me that Austin had the best doctor they had doing his surgery. We then walked out into the waiting area.

It looked like a party. We had many friends and family who were there for us. I can't even begin to tell you how comforting that was! We were absolutely not alone on this journey, that's for sure! I sat among our friends and family in one of the recliners to endure the long night of waiting. Thankfully, while in the waiting area, they gave me frequent updates on Austin's progress, which helped ease my worry. I called Lucy and Chloë, who were having a girls' night with my niece Jessica, and tried to reassure them as best I could. I could tell they were worried, but I was so glad they got to be with Jess, one of their favorite people! At around eleven o'clock, the waiting room attendant told me that they were moving him to recovery, and the surgeon would be out to talk to me soon.

When I met with Dr. Foster, he said that the surgery went very well, but that Austin was a very sick man. He said that he couldn't believe how stoic Austin was prior to surgery given how very sick he was. He told me to be prepared for a very bumpy ride and that Austin would probably get a lot sicker before he got better because of the toxins throughout his abdominal cavity. Infection was probable. I told him that we had a small country praying for him and that he was going to pull through this, come hell or high water. That is such a weird saying. I wouldn't want hell to come, although I felt many times that it already had, and high water just meant that we would need a boat or something. Anyway, I was holding on to the hope that Austin would be okay. Would he make it through this?

God only knows ...

Chapter 37

Austin's Recovery at the Hospital

Once we were told that Austin was in recovery, most of our wonderful support group went home. We first held hands in a big circle for a prayer. This gave me so much peace and comfort. My sister Anne, my friend Becky, Rae, and Austin's mom, Sue, stayed until Austin was taken to his room. The wait seemed like forever! At one point, Becky and I went to the restroom. I was in a bit of a mess myself, literally. My ulcers were bleeding like crazy, and it was dripping down my legs! I always wore a pad, but it had soaked through.

I remember a few people saying to me over the last several days, "This will be a new role for you taking care of Austin. Maybe it's what you need?"

They weren't kidding, but I'm not sure it's what I needed! I just kept thinking, *It would be really nice if I wasn't sitting in a pool of my own blood. God? Can You hear me now? Could You possibly heal my ulcers, since I'm now going to be the nurse? A nurse shouldn't have to watch her own blood drip while caring for someone else's!*

I don't think we got to see Austin until one in the morning. I will never forget it though. He looked like he was in so much pain. It was horrible! Rae and Austin's mom talked to him briefly and then I was alone with him.

He repeated over and over through tears, "Please don't leave me! Please don't leave me!"

Really? I was not prepared for that at all. Are you kidding me? It was the most difficult goodbye yet.

I walked out of his room and went to talk to his nurse. She promised me that he wouldn't remember any of it and that she would call me immediately if there was a need. Seriously? I was supposed to leave my husband who was in so much pain, scared, crying, and begging me not to leave? I don't think I'd ever seen Austin cry. I'm talking full-on crying … not just tears in his eyes or a little welling up. He was literally sobbing. God? Is this part of my miserable, on-going, totally sucky, never-ending journey? Well, I don't like it! I am a much better patient, and Austin is a much better nurse! I already feel like I am horrible at my new role, and to be honest, he is not very good at his! I'm pretty sure I never begged him through tears not to leave me, and I know that I never made peace with God and gave up!

I peeked back into his room, and he was asleep, or so it appeared. I had to do it. I had to leave. I hadn't seen Lucy and Chloë all day, and they needed me to be home. They needed to feel my hugs. Austin would understand when we got past this very difficult day. I knew he would. I walked out to find Anne and Becky and told them that we could leave. Those dear women hugged me and said nothing. It was perfect, because at this time, there were no words. No words could ease my pain, and no words would give me comfort, and these very important women in my life knew that. Thank goodness!

We got to the van and proceeded to leave the hospital. It was strange. We started the day at a different hospital, which had been our temporary home for a few days, and now we were driving away from Austin's new temporary home. It was one-thirty in the morning, and the streets were empty. There were no traffic jams on what was usually a very busy street and no red lights because they were all flashing yellow. I just stared ahead. It wasn't until we were rounding a corner in the country between the hospital and our small town that I felt a flash of energy.

Anne yelled, "Becky, do you see the deer? Do you see it? Becky!"

"Oh my," was Becky's very calm response as she just missed hitting the deer in the road. "That wouldn't have been good."

This actually made me laugh.

It was the kind of laugh after you have been through something horrible, and you realize, *Whatever! Throw it at me! I can handle it because I already have! I am strong, and I am not giving up! Do You hear me, God? Do you hear me, world? Team Oliver can do this, and we really, truly are!*

Would there be even more mountains to climb in our future?

God only knows …

Chapter 38

Our Vacation at the Hospital

I got home, went in to hug and kiss both girls, and then tried to get to bed myself. At 4:00 a.m., I was still lying there awake. I wonder how many years a person can go without sleep? I literally felt like I had been up for years. I decided to call Austin's nurse. I'm sure the nurses love it when crazy nut-job family members call in the middle of the night. Like they aren't busy enough! Hey, she'd made the mistake of telling me that I could. She told me that he was doing as expected. I, of course, took that to mean he was on the verge of death. She then tried to reassure me that he was doing just fine. I asked her when the doctors usually came in to do their rounds. She said that sometimes it was as early as six, which was all I needed to hear. I was up and out of the house by five. What was I thinking? I wasn't. I just knew that I needed to be there.

This was how the next several days would go. I would leave the house by five in the morning, and I would stay by Austin's side until about nine at night. On one of the first nights leaving the hospital by myself, I got out to the parking ramp and had no idea where I had parked. I called Becky bawling. She calmly talked to me while I went from floor to floor. I kept hitting my lock button to see if I could hear my horn. Eventually I found it on the fourth floor. I was a mess and fading fast.

Unfortunately, stress did not help my stomach issues either. At this point, we were about one week into this, and I hadn't been able to keep anything down. This means I was not eating, I was not sleeping, and I was bleeding from the ulcers down under. It was not pretty. I needed an intervention.

When Austin's hospital vacation began, we had a different person stay at our house with us every night. The list included my nieces, Marie, Elisa, and Jessica; my sisters, Anne, Lee, and Joy; my sister in-law, Diane; and my mom. On the night that my sister in-law stayed, it was about the fourth night of Austin's hospital stay. I couldn't sleep, so I got up and decided to write. I wrote to God and then I made lists.

Everyone and their mother was asking how they could help us, and all I could ever muster up to say was, "Please pray!"

Well, on this night I would make a list of what we needed help with besides prayer. Our camper was still packed, and it needed to be cleaned out; our house was a mess, our girls needed to be carted places and brought to the hospital for visits; our lawn needed to be mowed; our dentist appointments needed to be canceled; and my hair needed to be combed. Really, I'm not kidding. It was a snarly mess! There were many other things on the list. I really needed someone to help me figure out how to eat and keep it down. I was at 114 pounds and fading fast. Have I mentioned that I started this journey at 154 pounds? If we didn't have an intervention soon, I was going to have a room next door to Austin's.

I left the list with Diane that morning. She read it and then helped to get it done. She shared it with my brother, Jack, who got on the horn, and they got all the stuff checked off my list. I guess that day in church they prayed for us and then Lucy and Chloë sang the song, "Lord Prepare Me to Be a Sanctuary."

Are you kidding me? You are so amazing, God! Thank You for preparing our girls like only You could. I know that I curse You, and then I praise You, and then I go back to cursing. I am a perfect example of a very imperfect person. My flaws are right out there for all to see. But really, thank You for surrounding us with love, courage, and hope. Who gives an eight- and a ten-year-old the courage to sing in front of the church while their daddy is fighting for his life and their mom is not far behind? You do! You give us exactly what we need when we need it. Thank You! Thank You for the journey, the people in our lives to lift us up, and the strength to keep us moving forward in faith!

After Jack got my list, he came with Anne to the hospital that same afternoon. They told me that I was going home. No questions asked. Up until this point, I did not feel like I could leave Austin. Who was going to advocate for him if I wasn't there? Who was going to be his ears? Anyone who knows Austin knows that he cannot hear to save his life, so I needed to be there. My siblings decided that, for my own health, I needed to leave the hospital in the evening. They decided I could be here every day, but every night someone was going to come and sit with Austin so that I could go home. I tried to argue, but I didn't have it in me, and they weren't giving me an option. I also knew they were right. I said goodbye to Austin that first evening. I bawled, but I did leave with Anne while Jack stayed with Austin. Anne and I went straight to see Dr. Tom. He met us at his office on a Sunday night, no questions asked.

He took one look at me and said, "I'm not going to even ask you how you are doing. I can see. You are not doing very well!" He gave me a chiropractic adjustment and then he just talked. He said, "You need to listen to me. Austin is going to pull through this. It's not going to be easy, and he has a long road ahead, but he is going to be okay. You, I'm afraid, are not going to make it unless you take care of yourself. Austin is pretty sick, but your situation is nothing to mess with either. You are fading away to nothing before our eyes. You are starting to look gray, and if you got caught in even a slight breeze, you would blow away. We have to get you something that you can keep down so you can gain some strength. I am worried about you!"

He gave me a couple of different protein drinks to try and said he had more if those didn't work. He told me to come see him tomorrow and every day after that if I needed. He gave me a hug, which was huge. Anybody who knows Tom Kennedy knows that he is not a hugger! He did knock some sense into me, that's for sure!

We developed a new system. I would leave in the morning for the hospital and stay until someone relieved me at night. On one of Austin's particularly difficult days, he asked to not have any visitors. He didn't even want to see the girls. I granted his wish. When I got home that night, which would have been about his fifth night away from home, I got home before the girls were dropped off. I barely got in the door when I saw Anne pull up with Chloë. Right after that, Lucy was dropped off by Barb, who was a good friend but also the mom of one of Lucy's dear friends.

I was absolutely exhausted. I took one look at the girls and could see that they were too! Anne and I and the girls stood in front of our garage. I asked them about their day. Lucy couldn't even talk.

She started to say, "It was fine ..." and then she broke down crying. Actually, it was very sad, heart-wrenching sobs.

She tried to speak through her tears, "Mom, you promised we could see him every day!"

She was sobbing and then Chloë started too. I just hugged them and stared ahead like a zombie. Anne was crying too. My eyes were empty; there were no more tears. None. I told the girls that I was so very sorry. I just kept repeating that I was sorry over and over while hugging them. I told them that it was wrong that I didn't keep my promise. I just kept holding them with what little strength I had. Chloë finally broke the silence.

She said very simply but with Chloë-like force, "Don't ever do it again! We are going to see him tomorrow!"

I told them that their dad was not feeling well that day, but that we needed to consider their feelings too. I asked them to forgive me and made sure they knew I felt horrible.

We went into my bedroom, crawled under the covers, and hugged. We hugged for a very long time without speaking at all. They needed to see that I was strong and that I would listen to them. They were so worried and rightfully so! This was the guy who took care of them and now they were stuck with sick old Mom. It was no wonder that they were freaked. Our girls had learned to go with the flow and roll with the punches, but they needed to feel heard, they needed to feel safe, and they needed to see their daddy every day!

They asked if we could pray. Just as we started, Anne came in the room. Lucy invited her to get into bed with us.

She said, "Come on, Anne. We are going to pray. It always helps."

The look on Anne's face was if she was going to melt with love and compassion for all three of us ... she looked as tired as we did. This life was taking a toll on many people ... definitely not just the four of us!

This was my prayer on that night: "Dear Jesus, we need You. We need You to help us get through this. Lucy and Chloë need You, and they need to see their daddy. Help us to remember that every single day. Please help Daddy to heal and get stronger. Please help all of us get through this really hard time. We know that You are always with us. Help us to remember that. We love You, Jesus! Amen!"

Would Austin be at the hospital forever? It sure felt like it, but …

God only knows …

Chapter 39

Austin's Homecoming

After spending almost two weeks in the hospital, Austin was finally coming home. This was exciting but also scary. How was I going to care for him? How was I even going to help him get out of bed? He had a very large abdominal incision with dressings that needed to be changed as well as the ostomy bag ... oh my!

Thankfully, one of my best friends, Jane, was more on top of things than me. Aside from always being just a phone call away, she thought of everything! She had come to our house the night before with several meals to put in our freezer as well as a handrail that we could put on the side of our bed. This would allow Austin to grab on to something other than me, who would just fall face first on top of him if he tried to use me as a rail.

She and I, but mostly Jane, set the handrail up. At one point, we had to lift our king-size mattress to get the apparatus securely under it. This was a pee-in your-pants kind of laughing moment. Ladies, you know what I'm talking about. Jane is strong, but I was as weak as they come at this particular time in my forty-three years of life. She kept telling me not to lift, that she would do it, and then she would catch me trying.

She would say, "Yo, idiot with the bleeding crotch. Stop! I got this!" and then she would lift it maybe an inch.

We started laughing, and we just couldn't stop. It was exactly what the doctor ordered. Laughter truly was the best medicine, and in the end, she got it all set up!

The next morning, I was so excited. It was like Christmas! The house was totally clean thanks to our dear friend Liz. The refrigerator was stocked, thanks to many people. We were ready! The girls and I were beyond ecstatic to bring Austin home. I made the drive into the city and proceeded to the hospital. I got into the ramp, pulled my ticket, and drove in to find a parking space. At that very moment, it hit me. What was I doing? I had been to this hospital too many times to count in the last four years for my own surgeries. However, this was not the hospital where Austin was. Are you kidding me? This would explain how tired I really was. I had driven to the wrong hospital. At first, I thought, this would be my own little secret, but I ended up telling him what I had done. He said, "Just another story for the book you're going to write someday." How did he know?

After my little detour, when I finally got to Austin's room, I walked in to him enjoying a visit with our dear friends Chuck, Mary, and Ted. I entered the room to their greetings and laughter. Chuck had a way of always bringing a smile to my husband's face. I was not, however, prepared for what Austin had to tell me. He said that his blood counts were not good and that he had a fever. He told me that he wouldn't be going home. I looked at him, paused, and then excused myself from the room. I needed a moment. I walked out into the waiting area, sat down, and bawled. This journey was a roller-coaster of highs and lows. Actually, it seemed like it was sometimes just lows and lowers. This was a lower for me. Not coming home? But I had promised the girls. When would I learn? Stop promising anything! That was just stupid! Nobody knows what the next day, or should I say, the next hour will bring. God only knows … *idiot*! Get a clue from the future title of your own book!

When we got the news that Austin would not be coming home, we were totally bummed. However, we were so glad that they caught the infection before we left. Austin had two fairly large abscesses in his abdominal cavity. Unfortunately, this meant that he would require another procedure. He would have ultrasound-guided tubes placed in his sides. The tubes would drain these lovely pockets of pus. Isn't that great terminology? Pockets of pus are just the thing you don't want to come home with, especially when your nurse was me!

It was quite unreal what modern medicine could do. It was also unreal what modern medicine couldn't do, but that's a different chapter. Anyway, Austin ended up with two tubes, one on each side that had bags on the end of them from which we would have to drain the pus. This was in addition to his ostomy and ostomy bag. He was my very own bagger.

Since Austin does all the grocery shopping at our house, I would be taking on another new role. I would become the shopper and probably the bagger too! We would both be baggers … woohoo! Can you believe all that we have shared as a couple? He put a vacuum on my area down under and got to pack and unpack my hema-son-of-a-bitch-toma wound, and I got to help change his poophole bag and drain his pus bags. Now that's love! We actually thanked God often for these activities that we got to share together. I'm not even kidding, people! Our marriage was better because of it, no doubt.

This all meant another couple of nights at the Hospital Hilton. Was it the worst thing in the world? No. Did we want him home sooner? Yes. Did we want him home healthy? For sure! We just rolled with the punches and handled it with as much grace as we could muster. For all four of us, our grace-mustering abilities were perfect at this point! There were only a few swear words mixed in for good measure. However, we were mostly just grateful.

On Austin's actual homecoming day, my brother, Jack, and our good friend Will drove into the hospital together to help bring us home. You would not believe the actual amount of medical stuff we had to bring home with us. It filled up the back of our van.

I remember when they got to Austin's room, Will took one look at Austin and said, "Good to see you, buddy! What's left of you, that is."

Austin had lost a ton of weight. He was almost skeletal. We both were. We were kind of a scary pair, but we were a strong pair! Stronger together, that's for sure! Jack and Will helped get us out of there, and they drove us home.

I will never forget the smile on Austin's face as we drove into our town. He was so happy to be coming home! As we got closer to our house, we noticed signs that had been put up! It was our very own welcome home party posted on trees and telephone poles along the way. The encouragement and love we felt was incredible! When we got to the top of our street, there was a group of people cheering! It was all for Austin! It was the most heartwarming feeling! As we pulled down our hill toward our house, there was a huge welcome-home sign on our garage, and all three of our girls were waiting outside, along with Rae's boyfriend at the time, Ben, who is now her husband. I'm pretty sure Austin had tears. I know I sure did!

Would our lives now turn around now that Austin was home?

God only knows ...

Chapter 40

A Homecoming Party in the 'Hood?

Having Austin home was a new balancing act, and sometimes it tipped us right over. On his very first night, after I
got the girls to bed, cleaned up the kitchen, cleaned up my own
bleeding mess, and drained his pus bags, we finally got to bed
ourselves. We looked at each other, smiled, thanked God for all
our blessings, and then went to sleep.

On this night, sleep came fast. However, within a couple of
hours, we were awakened to a party at the house behind ours.
This was our new normal. For the last two weeks while Austin
had been in the hospital, our backyard neighbors had hosted
a loud drinking party every single night at around two in the
morning when the bars closed. Unfortunately, our bedrooms
were on the same side of the house as their patio. You could practically jump onto the roof of their house from our deck. They
were that close. We live in a lovely, family filled neighborhood
where these kinds of parties do not ever happen. This house,
however, was being rented by two guys who liked to drink,
swear loudly at the top of their lungs, and party all night long!

On Austin's first night home, we were awakened by very
loud swearing. My first mistake was helping Austin get up. I
told him that I would handle it. I walked out onto our back deck
and the scene was very disturbing, to say the least.

I watched one guy trying to strangle another guy while yelling, "I'm going to f-ing kill you!"

All this while the drunk crowd cheered on. Holy buckets! What did I think I was going to do from my deck above them in my pjs? I ran back inside, grabbed the phone, and called the police.

I soon realized that Austin was nowhere to be found. You have got to be kidding me! I looked out the window, and in the middle of the street I saw my sick husband carrying his pus bags and walking very slowly toward the neighbor's house. Really? At least I'd had the sense to call the police. What did my three-bagged, skeletal husband think he was going to do?

Thankfully, the police were already driving down the hill. I told them not to use lights or sirens because the party was sure to scatter, which is exactly what happened. The police ended up talking to my very sick husband in the middle of the street while the renter/strangler/very drunk neighbor hid in the bushes across the street.

Nobody got a ticket, but the party at least was over for the night. Austin came back into the house. We drained his bags, changed his ostomy bag, and climbed back into bed by three-thirty in the morning. By four-thirty, we were back up because Austin needed pain medication. To tell you the truth, so did I! As I was trying to help Austin get up, I started to feel faint. I broke out into a cold sweat and started to see sparkles like never before. I told him he needed to lie back down, which wasn't easy with his abdominal incision, but I was afraid I was going to fall on him, and he was only halfway up at that point. I did fall, but thankfully, it was on the recliner next to our bed. I quickly put my head between my knees. Seriously? Was this really happening? Yes, it was. Oh joy. By the time I got my bearings back, I was drenched in sweat. I got up to help Austin, and we looked at each other and just smiled. We both knew that all of this was out of our control and we needed help.

After getting Austin his meds and resituating ourselves back into bed, I couldn't sleep. I decided that I needed to ask for help. The neighbors next door were too much for us to handle on our own. I wrote an email to our surrounding neighbors. I explained the situation that had occurred and what had been occurring every night for the last two weeks. I asked them to please help us. We were in over our heads, and I couldn't have my husband out in the street in the middle of the night dealing with it.

Given the awesome neighborhood that we live in, by mid-morning we had a crew at our house. They met up in our front yard and decided that they needed to approach the older of the two gentlemen who lived at the house. I had learned that it was an uncle and his nephew who were both pretty young. According to Rick and John, our next-door and across-the-street neighbors, the uncle was a very nice guy when he was sober. Rick and John went to talk to him. I guess the conversation went well, and he was very sorry. He didn't know that we were in the middle of a health crisis, and he promised that there would be no more parties. Rick and John also made it clear to him that this was not the kind of neighborhood that would allow it. It takes a village, people, and sometimes you need to ask for help when you are in over your head.

I certainly don't want to disregard alcoholism as being a very serious disease. If that was what our neighbor was dealing with then we would and did pray for him to get help. Our issue was with the combination of alcohol at two in the morning while attempting to murder somebody while we were in the middle of our own nightmare. I know, call us crazy on our first night back home while Austin was trying to recover from his near-death situation. Would we need more help in the future?

God only knows …

Chapter 41

Did Austin Do Well Now
That He Was Home?

The initial days of having Austin home were kind of eventful, as we were getting used to the kind of care that he needed. Unfortunately, on the first day that the nurse came, I had my own appointment with Dr. Steve. Our friend Will offered to come and be with Austin and take notes while the nurse was here. This was a total "God thing" because it was not only extremely helpful, it opened up a conversation that we had with Will about his grandfather having an ostomy. We were coming to find out that this wasn't such a rare medical condition for people to have, which helped make us feel less alone.

I went to my appointment with Dr. Steve, and we did the usual, "How's it going?" routine, knowing full well that it wasn't going well. This exchanging of pleasantries in the midst of our storm was comforting, however untrue it was. I had called Steve a few days after Austin was at the hospital to explain to him what was going on. He was in shock like everyone else.

I remember him saying, "No way, but Austin was so healthy! Have you guys ever considered checking out your house? Maybe there is something in there that is causing all of it. It's worth a shot."

One of the first things that he said at this appointment was, "I really think the house check is a good idea."

I told him that Dr. Tom was saying the exact same thing. We were going to start with a radon check and then go from there.

As far as the rest of the appointment, he did another lovely pelvic exam, which revealed the same three nasty bleeding ulcers that had been there for years. We talked about them looking worse than ever and that the stress of everything and the addition of my new, very active role as Austin's nurse was probably playing a part. He said that he was concerned about my weight and wanted to know what I was doing to get a handle on that, and then we said goodbye until he would check me again the next month. He also said that we were in his prayers. This meant a lot given that we had not really talked a ton about our faith with him.

I got home to find that Will had everything under control. He asked about my appointment, and I said that it was horrible as usual, but that it was good to see Steve. I did tell him about getting our house checked.

He gave that skeptical look, like only Will can, and then said, "It's worth a try. It's not like you have anything else to lose. Well, you do, but … let's not go there!"

He also mentioned that Zorro, as some of our friends like to call Austin, seemed really out of it. Thankfully, Will took great notes during the appointment with the nurse. We can't reiterate enough how fortunate we were to have the friends that we did and the support that we had. We were truly blessed during this time in so many ways, and we have never forgotten it!

Austin's demeanor, however, was very concerning. He couldn't seem to wake up … ever. He would sleep twenty-four seven if I let him. I know what surgery does to a person's body and how utterly exhausted you feel, but Austin's energy level seemed a little extreme. He wasn't even taking pain meds by now, so we knew that this wasn't the problem. His abdominal incision also started to look really funky. That's another great medical term that I have picked up over the years. He had a very long, bloody trail of funkdom that went from his belly button on down.

I love the word *funkdom*, even though I made it up. I think it describes many things, like when I feel depressed I think of it as my "blue fog of funkdom." It's a real thing, people!

We ended up calling his surgeon's office. They got Austin right in to look at his incision. They said it looked like it was starting to get infected and was opening a bit. They cut into it and drained out the nasty part. They put him on an antibiotic and sent us on our way. They also reassured us that his exhaustion was entirely common, and we should not be worried. His body had been to war and was just fighting its way back. His energy level would come back in time. Why did my gut tell me that this wasn't the problem?

God only knows …

Chapter 42

How Safe Is the Air We Breathe?

Our radon check came back totally fine, so I called Dr. Tom. He said that he had some other ideas, but he would like to come out to the house and check some things himself. We happened to not be home when he came, which was fine. We totally trusted Tom and just gave him our garage code. He called us after he had been there for about an hour.

He said to me, "I think I have figured out your problem, but I need you to call the gas company. It appears to me that your master bedroom and bath are contaminated with something. The worst area is at the head of your bed, but the whole room contains something toxic."

Wait, what? What did this even mean? Was this even possible? I handed Austin the phone, and Tom told him the same thing. We totally trusted Tom with our lives, so we really didn't even ask him any questions. We didn't ask how he knew, we didn't ask if it was anywhere else in the house, we didn't even ask what he had for breakfast. Like I said, we trusted him with our lives. He was simply amazing!

We got home and called the gas company right away. A technician came out immediately because that's what they do if there is some suspicion of an issue. The girls and I stayed clear and let Austin handle everything. He followed him all around the house inside and out. I doubted that they would find anything, but then I remembered, "It's Dr. Tom. He's always right." What if they did find a problem, and it answered all our health issues? I couldn't even go there because it's very hard to get your hopes up and then have them flipped on end.

I did, however, say a quick prayer. "God? Yeah, it's me again. Please help them find whatever it is they are supposed to and please let it help us. Amen!"

After the gas guy left, Austin came to me and said, "Honey, we had a very significant gas leak. I don't know what this means, or if it has anything to do with our health issues, but wow. What if it does? It's already fixed. It took him less than two minutes to fix it."

I said right away, "How long has it been there? What do you mean 'significant?' Shouldn't we have been able to smell it? There is no way. Seriously? Do you really think that maybe it could be the answer? Oh my goodness … what if this is what we have been praying for?"

Austin tried to slow my racing thoughts down. He grabbed my shoulders, looked into my eyes, and said, "We don't know for sure, but it feels like it might be our answer. Let's just wait and see. Let's call Dr. Tom back, but then let's keep this to ourselves. The gas guy said the leak could have been there since we built in 2005. About right when you started having symptoms. I have a feeling it was never fully tightened from the very beginning. I have smelled that odor occasionally, but certainly not all the time. It's the fitting where the gas comes into the house. I think our house is so airtight that maybe the bad fumes are coming in and then concentrating in our bedroom because the piping is right underneath there. We have to call Tom."

I called him immediately. "Hello, Tom? Are you sitting down? We have, or I should say, had, a significant gas leak."

"I knew it! This is your answer. I just know it. Let's see how you feel in a couple of weeks. I think this is it!"

"The guy said it could have been there from when we built. That's six years! We possibly have been living with this for six years! I have felt like I have had the flu for six years! Oh my goodness, Tom … do you really think this could be our answer? If it is, we owe you with our lives!"

"I have been waiting for this day for a long time, and the only thing you owe me is for you to get well. I will finally be able to sleep knowing that."

"If it's really it, Tom, I am going to get this body out on a bike. I am actually going to put this crotch on a bike! Lucy and Chloë don't even know that I know how to ride!"

"Just keep me posted on your progress, okay?"

"For sure! I just saw Dr. Steve and my ulcers were actually worse. Wouldn't it be something if they improved? That will be our proof, Tom!"

"You feeling better will be our proof!"

"We love you, Tom Kennedy!"

"I love you guys too!"

Was this the answer?

God only knows …

Chapter 43

My Next Appointment with Dr. Steve

Austin and I didn't mention our gas leak to many people in that first month. We just tried to remain calm and observe our symptoms. We did start to feel better, but we didn't know if it was real or in our heads. We had a lot of doubt and were going forward with cautious optimism. My first appointment with Dr. Steve would be the test.

He walked in, we did the, "How's it going?" routine, and I said to him, "It's going good, Steve, and I'm not lying this time."

"Really? What's going on?"

"Well, remember when you said we should check out our house? The radon came back normal. So Dr. Tom came out to our house. He went through the entire place top to bottom, inside and out. He discovered that we had something toxic in our master bedroom."

"He did? What was it?"

"Well, it was a natural gas leak."

"No way, really? How do you know, and couldn't you smell it?"

"That's what I said! Apparently, since we built, the fitting on the gas piping going into our house was never tightened. We called the gas company, they came right out, found the leak, and fixed it immediately. The gas guy told Austin that it was pretty significant. I'm a little freaked, Steve, because I actually do feel better, and I don't seem to be bleeding as much."

"Are you serious? Do you really think that it was the answer?"

"I don't want to say, but maybe. We don't want to be let down, so we are trying to stay guarded, but I think it might be. I'm trying to be cautious because I don't want to be dissappointed."

"Well, let's do an exam and see what it looks like."

He really couldn't believe it. After years of staring at these ulcers, one was not even visible, the other was barely visible, and the third was much improved. Are you kidding me? Was this really happening? Steve was in shock and so was I. I knew that I felt better, but I was too afraid that it wasn't going to last forever. I was too afraid that it would be just one of those "Sorry, joke's on you! Just kidding! Continue suffering! Your nightmare continues, and you're still sick!" kind of stories.

Dr. Steve just stood up and stared at me. It felt like several minutes of both of us in disbelief. Could this really be our answer?

Steve said something like, "If I hadn't been witnessing all of it for so long, I'm not sure I would believe it myself. This is completely crazy! You need to write a book or something!"

After several long years of feeling like garbage, I actually had proof that it was over. This was huge, this was unbelievable, and this was the answer to prayer!

I think I hugged Steve when I left his clinic that day. I walked out of there for the very first time feeling like a walking miracle. I'm pretty sure he was feeling the same way.

Can you believe it? I was not a nutjob! I was not anorexic, and I did not have bulimia. I was not depressed and doing this to myself in my sleep. I, along with Austin, Lucy, Chloë, and Cooper, were being poisoned, and we had proof.

My issues seemed to be the most significant. I had endured ten-plus surgeries. I had permanent stomach damage. I was out of work for well over two years. I lost a lot of my hair and a lot of weight. I developed a very large hiatal hernia. I had wounds that would not heal. And, one of the hardest pills to swallow was I lost my daughters' childhoods, which I could never get back. We even lost friends along the way and became somewhat isolated.

Austin had three surgeries. He lost part of his colon. He had an ostomy. He retired early, and he aged very fast. Lucy lost her tonsils and adenoids. She had two surgeries. She had constant sinus infections. And she couldn't read, write, or do math! Chloë had constant stomach issues. She struggled every day to sleep. And she couldn't read, write, or do math! Cooper pretty much hated coming in the house, and when he did come in, he was lethargic beyond measure. Remember, he was the dog we couldn't catch if he got outside without a leash. Would the gas leak have any permanent effects?

God only knows …

Chapter 44

Life Afterward

How do I even begin to explain what life was like after the gas leak was found and then fixed? For the first few months, it was a little like walking on thin ice. Was it going to crack? Was this some kind of joke, and we really weren't going to heal? After six years of horrible craziness, you have to admit, it could cause some skepticism. At least it did for me—Austin tended to be more optimistic. I like to say I'm the realist bordering on slightly suspicious. What can I say? Non-healing vaginal ulcers, a larger-than-life hematoma, constant brain zaps, and throwing up for years might do that to a person.

Initially, in our post-gas-leak life, let's call it Team Oliver's PGL, it was just the physical changes that we noticed. Calling it the PGL makes it sound like we were in some kind of professional league. The only problem was that this league didn't come with income, fame, or fortune, but thankfully it came with a mighty God combined with *big* faith. If I couldn't be in the NFL as a punter, then this was the best league to be in, that's for sure! At any rate, one of the biggest PGL changes for Austin was that he woke up. He no longer felt like he was in a fog twenty-four seven, his incisions actually healed, and he adapted to life with an ostomy.

Austin's energy level also picked up pretty fast, and he quickly resumed his incredible work ethic. I'm pretty sure he was doing a construction side job within a month's time of the leak being fixed, even with his ostomy bag, and he handled it all with amazing grace, like only Austin Oliver can! Our good friend Bob, who we like to call the Torch, can attest to that. He had the pleasure of working underneath Austin's ladder on one job. Let's just say the ostomy bag adhesive didn't hold on this particular ninety-degree day. Poor Torch!

As for Lucy and Chloë, there were physical changes that occurred that we didn't even realize were chronically there. Lucy's sinuses cleared up, the dark circles under her eyes went away, and she slowly came alive. Chloë, who we thought just had a nervous stomach, didn't complain as much. Her tummy problems became a lot less of an issue. She, like Lucy, gradually started to wake up over the next six months. Even our dog, Cooper, experienced a significant change to his life and behavior. For the very first time since we got him, he did not have to be taken outside on a leash because he came into the house willingly. We'd thought we'd just had a strange dog that loved to be outside and hated to come in. No, we had a dog that knew he didn't want to be in a house that made him feel like a zombie. I'm telling you, people, "Listen to your pets!"

As for me, the ulcers going completely away was my biggest and most obvious initial change. I no longer felt like I had to hold my pelvis when I moved, and I could sit without feeling like I was going to die. However, one of the symptoms that I was most excited about not having was feeling like I had the flu all the time. This constant nausea was not in my head, and I did not have an eating disorder!

Austin would ask me frequently in the first few months of not being gassed, "How do you feel? Do you still feel nauseous all of the time, or is that completely gone?"

My answer was always, "Yes, and I can't even believe it!"

We, like everybody else around us, thought it was just me. I seemed to be the only one in our family who was sick. I was the weird, weight-losing, throwing-up-constantly, freakish non-healer. I was the one who had stumped every doctor from the Faraway Clinic to the Clinic Faraway. Were we thankful that Austin had gotten sick? We actually were! Had Austin's colon not ruptured out of the blue, we would have continued down that very unhealthy, depressing, nonhealing, very sucky and completely mysterious road. Did we still have very difficult days ahead? Absolutely, without a doubt, but we knew that God would see us through those!

Within the year of the gas leak being fixed, Austin would have to endure two more surgeries. His surgery to take down the ostomy was seven months after his initial emergency surgery, and he had to have a hernia, caused from the initial surgery, repaired, eight months after that. Those days were very hard for all four of us. Some of the emotions of that very scary time we'd had seven months prior had never been dealt with, and the emotional scars from that time were certainly not healed. The tears and fears seemed to flow out of all of us when Austin had to prepare and endure his second surgery. We were anxious and not thrilled to be thrown back into recovery mode.

If you think about it, this mode is one that some people never deal with in their entire lives. It isn't something that you become good at, and it's one that we would love to never have to deal with again! The difference this time was that Austin came home after that surgery to a gas-free house. He didn't turn into a total zombie during his recovery, and he had no trouble healing, which was so refreshing! Who knew that recoveries could go smoothly? This was a first for us!

Getting back into the swing of living as healthy people was, believe it or not, challenging. We felt very isolated and quite alone. We had been out of the social scene for six years. Some people only knew us as the family that was going through crazy health stuff, but no one knew why. Some people resented all those years of feeling sorry for us and didn't really like us healthy. I'm not even kidding. It sounds kind of crazy to even write it, but it was true. Maybe you can relate to having someone in your life who can only be kind to you if they feel sorry for you? This was quite hard to deal with. We kept praying and giving it to Him, but I'm not going to lie, there were *many* tear-filled days.

The six years of being sick was a very long and lonely road at times, and the emotional toll that this took was hard to put behind us. When there weren't explanations for my health issues, and we thought it was just me, we know that people thought I was crazy, doctors thought I was crazy—I even wondered on more than one occasion. We experienced judgment, impatience, and isolation. It was hard to constantly try to answer questions that we didn't have answers to. "Why don't you heal normally? Why can't you eat? Do you have an eating disorder? What is wrong with you? Is there a diagnosis? Why would you have another surgery? Maybe you just need to get out more. Maybe you are just depressed. Maybe you should try this therapy, this drink, this supplement, or this drug. Have you prayed about it?"

Seriously, I'm not kidding. Life with an unexplained illness is hard, but dealing with people's questions and judgment is even harder!

I really don't know how else to explain it, but getting back to physical health and then emotional health was difficult. We spent a long time wondering if it was real and if getting and staying healthy would even last. Once again, we had to rely on faith and move forward over very tricky, emotion-filled days. Austin and the girls did a much better job of handling the journey than I did, in my opinion. Put it this way—I brought out the ugly cry on more than one occasion. One thing that I learned about myself during this journey was that I was not afraid of dying, but I had a very real fear of actually living. Ultimately, we got through it by focusing on all the kind people that God put in our lives. We remained grateful for the incredible blessings we had been given, and we put all our trust in His plan!

One of the most significant joys, post gas leak, was going to the girls' parent-teacher conferences in the spring of 2012. This was about seven months after the leak was fixed. Lucy and Chloë each got amazing grade reports that brought us to tears. Both girls could now read, and they absolutely enjoyed it! They each had test scores like they'd never had before! It was crazy to look at the charts where they show you your child's growth over the years. Are you kidding me? Both of their growth charts for reading and math made *leaps* in the upward direction.

I remember saying to their teachers, "You mean, they don't have learning disabilities?"

The response from both of their teachers was, "No, they do not, and in fact, they are above average!"

This was a definite high for both me and Austin. We no longer had to think about getting them tutors or agonizing over how we could help them. Today, Lucy and Chloë read all the time and are above grade level. We have had to tell them on more than one occasion to "put the book down!" This was unheard of in our gas-leak days! They are also in the highest math groups, and they love school! Our nights of living in homework hell were becoming a memory. This was a far cry from where we were, and we are so grateful!

Did the gas leak have any permanent or long-lasting effects? We don't really know. How would we know if it took years off our lives? How would we know if things would be different for us physically had it never happened?

We do know that my stomach has yet to regain function

and, for now, I still have to take medicine to eat or I will get sick. Believe me, I've tried to go off it, and I pay the price right away! It could be that once your stomach is paralyzed from breathing chemicals like that twenty-four-seven, it never regains back function. We don't really know. I also don't think Austin's gut will ever be the same either. He most likely did not go through two abdominal surgeries and the subsequent trauma without permanent effects. The girls and Cooper, however, seem to have totally bounced back, and they are all thriving, which is really the most important thing to me and Austin.

I do have to mention one incredible goal that has been achieved post gas leak. I have gotten this crotch onto a bike! I made it one of my goals once I started healing. Austin really enjoys road biking, and so I thought it would be incredible if we could enjoy it together. We entered a national contest to win a bike for me since they are quite expensive. I was a runner-up in the contest and ended up winning bike tools, a bike bag, bike lights, and a t-shirt. Seriously? It was hard to win all those things but not the bike. Kind of like it was hard to win the little Native American healer and not the all-inclusive vacation—just a joke, folks! Even though we didn't win the bike, we were able to cash in our coins, sold some things, and Austin did a few extra side jobs, which allowed us to purchase a road bike for me.

Even though this crotch of mine has some incredibly crazy scars, I was determined, and believe it or not, I have succeeded! I absolutely love to get out on my bike and ride the hills surrounding our 'hood. An hour of riding is about the maximum my screaming area down under will allow, but every time I get on the bike, I feel like I'm saying, "F- you, ten crotch surgeries! Here's to you, hema-son-of-a-bitch-toma straight from hell! And finally, here's to you f-ing gas leak!" Sorry about the f-bombs, but this was a major accomplishment that I do not take for granted and my area down under will never let me forget!

Unfortunately, as the post gas leak years have gone by, it has taken more of a permanent toll on my body. This is a pretty unreal part of the story and one, to this day, that I have a hard time wrapping my brain around. You see, because of the meds I must take in order to eat, I developed a condition in my breasts. Ultimately, this would lead to a double mastectomy. This is where you say, "Are you f-ing kidding me?" No joke here, folks! The gas leak took my breasts! Yes, it did! This was a very hard pill to swallow. I endured seven breast surgeries from February 2014 to December 2015. My left breast exploded twice prior to being removed. Yes, you read that right, it exploded! I'm not even kidding! I was in our bathroom after getting out of the shower. I was recovering from a breast surgery where they'd done a duct excision and removed several enlarged ducts, so I already had a compromised breast. At the time, they were ruling out cancer. At any rate, the pressure in the breast became so great that it literally exploded. We're talking full-on bloody fluid spraying all over our bathroom. Is that too graphic? Oh well, it was my experience. It was like something out of *The Exorcist*!

The even crazier thing was, not that an exploding breast wasn't crazy, but that Austin was also quite sick at the exact same time. He had severe, unexplained stabbing stomach pain. Because it was a Sunday, we ended up duct taping my breast and heading to the emergency room for him. We didn't really use duct tape, but you know, it does sound funnier. This was a totally weird scenario, but Austin needed help more than I did. It turned out that Austin was diagnosed with pancreatitis. At the ER they told him to go home and not eat for a week. Huh? That's how you treat that? Apparently, it is.

We got home from the hospital and then went to my breast

doctor the next day to deal with my exploding breast. The doctor glued the incision shut, and we thought I would be good to go. She was in total shock that this was even happening, by the way, and had never seen anything like it before. After being home not even twenty-four hours, the pressure gave way again and the glue didn't hold. Explosion number two occurred! No joke. You can't make this stuff up, people! Fluid would build up in my breast ducts, kind of like when a woman is nursing and gets engorged. My left breast would blow open, spray bloody fluid everywhere, and my right breast felt like it was going to as well. However, it just sprayed stuff out from the nipple and did not actually explode. Wait, is this too much to share? If you've read the book this far—this is nothing, right? I'm pretty sure if you know me, you will never look at me the same again, and I have to be okay with that. I'm good people, and believe it or not, I'm grateful for all of my life, exploding breasts included!

Back to the story. At the time of the exploding breasts and pancreatitis, I said to Austin, "I have this feeling in my gut, and it's not a good one. For peace of mind, I feel like we need to call the gas company. This latest health stuff is too weird."

Austin didn't bat an eye and said, "Let's do it."

We called, they came right away. You are not going to believe what they found and fixed! You got it. We had another gas leak, and this time it was in our furnace. Are we the only people in the world this happens to?

Was this the cause of Austin's pancreatitis attack? We don't know, but what we do know is that Austin healed up pretty quickly after that, and he has not had another attack since. The coincidence of that is just a little too hard to ignore, if you know what I mean.

My breasts were a different story. The incision held, but I still ended up with a double mastectomy. Again, because of the medication I must take to eat, fluid would continually build up in both breasts to the point of spraying around the room. Breast-feeding moms out there, you have to know what I'm talking about. It was like that, but really not the same—if you know what I mean. I was a post-hysterectomy, non-breast-feeding mom that had spraying and exploding breasts. This caused intense anxiety and was not very fun at all. To add insult to injury, I got shingles at the same time all this was happening. This was a definite valley road trip, and that blue fog of funk-dom took over my brain again for that time period.

Was this painful to go through? Extremely! Both physically and emotionally, losing my breasts because of a gas leak was very upsetting, but living without eating was kind of impossible, and dealing with the feeling that my breasts were going to explode at any given moment was horrible! So, removing my breasts was a no-brainer. We handled it the best way that we could—we relied on people to carry us through and gave it all to God.

It's all about perspective, folks! Did I ever imagine in my adult life when I first started teaching that this story would be mine? A hysterectomy, which led to many surgeries, a husband's ruptured colon and near death, my girls' childhood taken from them, exploding breasts that led to a double mastectomy, a gas leak that caused it all—no way in hell would I have told you that it was even possible or that I had the strength to endure. However, throughout it all, for some reason God gave me the will and courage to look past it … and I never had to look very far. I could see someone just down my street fighting for their life because of cancer. I knew of kids at school who were dealing with parents who had addictions. I could drive not far from my house and witness homelessness. Were their roads harder than mine? It always seemed like it. Hell, my burdens were nothing compared to what some people had to deal with. Again, it's perspective. I'm telling you, combined with faith and hope in something way bigger than yourself, it's what gets you through until tomorrow.

Was this post-gas-leak road an easy one to travel? God and Team Oliver know that it was not! Is anyone's life easy? No, absolutely not! I'm sure you can think about your own life and the storms you have endured. Life is hard, people! We know that we are not alone on that front. Do I know how anyone does this life without faith? I have no idea! Would our gas-leak experience help anyone else in the future?

God only knows ...

Chapter 45

How Does Anyone Live This Life Without Faith?

I cannot finish this book without talking about this very important question, and I have no idea what the answer is. We started this journey as church-going Christians. We talked the talk, but didn't really walk the walk. Our life was pretty easy. It's not that Austin and I hadn't been through difficult things, but I don't remember having to totally rely on faith to get through them. I actually thought I got through them because I was strong, I was in control, and I had incredible skills. I could not have been more wrong.

I am here to tell you that God gets total credit for everything. He gets credit for putting people in our lives to help us, support us, pray for us, and carry us when we were far too weak to walk on our own. He gets credit for giving us everything that we needed when we needed it. Without Him, and without faith, we would have been left in a pile, sobbing on the floor, and not moving forward ever! I didn't teach with three bleeding ulcers, with an administrator that wanted me gone, and throwing up daily without the help of a higher power. We didn't endure what we endured without relying on someone who is way bigger than we are. A person certainly doesn't find blessings in the storm without faith.

Do we believe that because Dr. Steve stuck with us and didn't ditch us that we were eventually healed? Do we owe Dr. Tom and give him credit for saving our lives? Yes, and yes, but God is the one who gave them their gifts, and God is the one who gets all the glory!! Can I get an *amen* to that?

We thank Him daily for our blessings, and we continue to feel humbled that He chose us to travel this very unique road. Austin and I are two high school teachers from a small town who were just trying to work hard and raise our daughters to be good people. Hell, we could be your next-door neighbor. We are that *ordinary* without an *extra* in front of that word. Why us? He only knows that answer … we have no clue. However, without Him, we are nothing, and if not for Him, this life really has no hope. Zilch, nada—a bit fat zero in the hope column! I'm pretty sure that hope goes into negative infinity mode. The math teacher in me had to put that in.

Every person can still experience joy and walk through life, but Austin and I have no idea how any of it makes any sense without faith. This is not it, people! This life is so insignificant compared to the life after this. We are all here for a purpose, and my very unimportant, small-town girl from Wisconsin self knows that part of my purpose was to live through this crazy story and write this book, even though I'm not a writer. My job is to spread a message of perseverance, faith, and hope. So, it's with a very grateful heart that I end our story. It's not important that my name is not really Kennedy Oliver. God knows who I am. Did you get the message and learn what you needed to?

I hope so, but God only knows …

A Doctor's Perspective

In February 2009 I received a call from my colleague, Dr. Kathryn Smith. "Steve, I am sending a patient to you who really needs your help. I am not sure what is going on with her, and she does not know where else to go. It seems like everyone is giving up on her. And by the way ... *she is not crazy!*" I am not sure if those were her exact words, but that was the basic gist of the conversation. I was flattered by the referral, and I was equally intrigued by the "she is not crazy." Maybe she is crazy, but crazy people need help too, and I am always up for the challenge. And what is crazy, anyway? "Of course, I will get her in right away," I said.

Kennedy and Austin arrived at our clinic, and after the nurse roomed them, she came to my office and gave me *the look*. It's that look of "good luck with this one." She handed me a bunch of records and stated, "Something is really wrong with her. Are you going to figure it out?" Now I was even more intrigued, and in my own modest and stubborn manner, replied, "I've got this." Of course I was going to figure it out. Someone had just not asked the right questions or delved deep enough into the medical history. They must have missed something. One of the best parts of my job is getting to play detective. You examine the record for clues, interview involved parties, and eventually, with a little bit of luck and determination, you solve the case. I was going to solve this case, but I was not going to be distracted by the reams of medical records. We were going to start from square one. Many persons had taken a shot at her case, but they must have missed something—something she said, something she did, something in her family history, or maybe even something in the home.

By the time Kennedy reached me, she had accumulated an impressive collection of notes, labs, and imaging studies. I would go through these later after I had heard her story. The best information you can get is straight from the patient, and first impressions can provide some of the most valuable pieces of information. I walked into the room, and I remember Kennedy sitting cockeyed on the exam table with Austin holding her hand as if to keep her from falling over. She could not sit directly on her bottom because of the pain. "Hey, Doc, are you a spiritual man, and can you help us?" Austin asked. She was obviously in significant discomfort, and after getting a brief history, I thought we should move quickly to the exam. I asked Kennedy to get undressed for the exam and left the room. Here was a young, relatively healthy-appearing female in significant distress from a simple and common procedure. Austin looked desperate. At the end of this first visit, Kennedy asked, "Now, you aren't going to ditch us, are you?" Without hesitation I responded, "Of course I will see this through until this is resolved." As I left the exam room, I quietly thought, *What am I getting myself into?* God only knew.

What started from that first exam was a medical odyssey not unlike the travels of Odysseus in Homer's *Odyssey*. Kennedy and Austin had embarked on what would become a long and complicated journey that certainly included time in the dark underworld. Their journey proved to be as psychological and spiritual as it was physical. On exam, Kennedy had an area of non-healing skin. We often see this after deliveries and gyne-cologic surgeries, and it is commonly referred to as granulation tissue. Usually this is simple to fix, and we patiently waited about five months for it to heal. Eventually, we went to the operating room for what should have been a very simple procedure to remove the granulation tissue and close her non-healing wound. The surgery went quite well, but when she returned for her post-operative check, the area looked as though we had never performed the surgery. In fact, it looked worse! Over time, the wound would evolve spontaneously into three separate areas of non-healing vaginal skin. At the same time, she had developed problems with chronic pelvic pain, unexplained weight loss, daily headaches, and bowel-related problems. I will never forget the visible decline that had taken place over this period. She would walk into clinic looking extremely tired, malnourished, and very weak. I knew something else must be going on, so we ventured further down the path into the dark medical underworld.

I helped to coordinate multiple referrals to specialists in gynecologic surgery, dermatology, plastics and reconstructive surgery, rheumatology, physical therapy, and nutrition, just to name a few. At the same time, Kennedy was pursuing chiropractic care and alternative medicine. Many extremely intelligent and well-meaning specialists did their best to figure out what was going on. But this was not always the case as she recounts her experience with Dr. Evil, who had little more to offer than a diagnosis of a crazy, tired, malnourished mother of young children who should wear oven mitts to bed so that she would stop scratching herself and opening up her surgical wounds in her sleep. Yes, a few thought she was crazy. Unfortunately, this is sometimes the reaction when you do not understand a confusing situation—to place blame and disconnect.

So, over the next year we made several more attempts to close the non-healing wound in novel ways. We felt that we had ruled out any condition or circumstance that would prevent normal wound healing, and the choice was to either live in excruciating pain or get the wound closed. This would produce one of the lowest points in her story involving a complication from surgery called a wound hematoma, or a collection of blood under the skin at the site of a surgery. Kennedy fondly referred to it as the hema-son-of-bitch-toma. This was a low point for me too. We got through it, barely. Beyond these failed attempts, there was nothing else to do except wait and pray that things would eventually change on their own. I had not cracked the case, and it was about to go into the cold case files forever! And that's when Austin got sick ... deathly sick.

When Kennedy told me about Austin, my reaction was one of incredulity. We had joked previously about whether their house was made using imported drywall (remember the issues surrounding Chinese imported drywall in the 2000s). It was the first time that it had occurred to all of us that something must not be right in their environment. Dr. Thomas Kennedy visited their home and fortunately discovered the gas leak. When the leak was fixed, everything changed. Austin made a full recovery, and Kennedy came into my clinic looking more healthy and energetic than I had ever seen before. More importantly, the wounds showed the first signs of healing that I had seen in two years. I brought her back to clinic twice over the following month and could hardly believe it—the wounds were closed, and her pain was almost gone. I would not have believed that the gas leak in the home could be the cause unless I had seen it for myself.

Kennedy and Austin's story is not really a story about medical problems and surgical wounds. Their story is about a journey in which a family discovers what really gets you through a life-altering experience. They all lived day-to-day with varying degrees of chronic illness that they could not explain. It affected their children, their dog, their activities, their moods, their emotions, and everything else that we take for granted when everything is going fine. Even in the depths of the underworld, they still found strength through their faith to keep going, believing that this must be happening for some reason, for some greater good. It is a testament to the faith and support required to get through the most trying of circumstances. I believe that Kennedy and Austin's story will save someone's life at some point. Maybe this is as simple as having the house checked for a gas leak. Or maybe the message is that you never give up— not on your family, your friends, your patients, your faith, or anyone who is mired in a bad situation that he or she cannot explain. I have learned more from my experience with Kennedy and Austin than they will ever understand.

Dr. Stephen Hopkinson, MD

A Message from Dr. Thomas Kennedy

The Oliver's ordeal started after moving into their new house. At the time no one had linked their problems to their environment. It was one dead end after another in terms of finding a solution. I had narrowed it down to something in the atmosphere, but then the question was what? I suspected the house, but I was totally convinced after Kennedy had called me and said Austin was in the hospital. I told her I needed to get in the house right away. Kennedy gave me the code to get into their garage so that I could go check it out when they weren't home.

Being trained in dowsing, I had checked all the rooms in the house with my instruments. The master bedroom being the predominant area of concern, I was picking up abnormal atmosphere readings about eighteen inches away from the wall. It ran right along the headboard and pillows where Kennedy and Austin slept. It was exciting that I had found the problem. However, we had yet to find the source. I dowsed the rest of the house, which proved to be negative. I then went outside and my readings picked up in intensity as I moved toward the gas meter.

After double-checking, I was sure the gas meter was the source, so I called Kennedy and told her to have the gas company come out and check for a leak. After the Oliver's story ran on local TV, I kept asking my front desk staff if anyone called telling me I was crazy. They quizzically asked why. You see, gas is heavier than air, and there's no way it would rise up like that.

Many had made this point. However, it wasn't the gas itself. It was one of the chemicals in the gas that caused the weakening in a part of the brain that was affecting the organ dysfunction in both Kennedy and Austin.

Through all the surgeries and medical mishaps, they did not lose their faith in God; in fact, it became even stronger. They could have fallen apart, blamed each other or God, but they did not. This, I feel, is a testament of their love for each other and the Lord.

I can only imagine the pain and suffering they had gone through. This ate away at my heart and was very difficult to watch as it was going on over many years. However, there was always a smile and a sense of perseverance with them while going through this hell on earth. Each visit I would ask Kennedy how she was doing, and she would smile and say, "I'm good." I told her I never thought I would find a better liar than myself.

This story is a story of love, perseverance, and an unyielding faith in our Lord.

Dr. Thomas Kennedy

Health History of the Olivers
from 2005–2016

9/05: The Olivers moved into a house that they built. Lucy and Chloë were two and four.

9/05–11/07: Health issues started: chest pain, flu-like symptoms, crazy gynecological issues, and chronic headaches for Kennedy.

Because of chronic sinus and strep issues, Lucy had her tonsils and adenoids out. She then had an emergency bleed that required a second surgery. The sinus issues continued, and she still had constant sinus infections.

Chloë had chronic stomachaches, and they were unable to find the cause. She also had sleep issues.

Lucy and Chloë both struggled in school. They both were in the lowest reading and math groups and had a hard time concentrating. The Olivers thought they had learning disabilities. They started down the road of tutoring.

11/21/07: Kennedy's first surgery. It was a laparoscopic supra-cervical hysterectomy to stop the constant bleeding.

2/19/08: Kennedy continued to bleed, which lead to a second opinion where the doctor said that she needed a second surgery to remove the cervix or she would continue to bleed. At this time, the doctor also recommended the excision of a non-healing perineal fissure.

4/13/08: Although Kennedy did not feel well, the doctor gave the okay to get back to regular activity. Her vaginal cuff ruptured during intercourse, which required an emergency surgery. This was an extremely difficult recovery. The rupture felt like an explosion inside her body—horrible! After this surgery, she struggled to keep down food and got sick almost every time she ate.

6/17/08: Kennedy's stitches from surgery #3 did not dissolve and became embedded and infected. It felt like many needles were stabbing her from within. This led to surgery #4, which was the removal of the non-reabsorbing sutures in the vaginal cuff.

7/08: After surgery #3 Kennedy also found out that she now had a very large hiatal hernia, which was not present prior to surgery #3. They consulted with a doctor who recommended she have that repaired surgically. They were told that this was causing her constant nausea. This resulted in going to the Clinic Faraway for a second opinion because Kennedy and Austin were freaked at the prospect of another surgery. Kennedy's hair was also falling out by the handfuls. She was throwing up daily and losing a lot of weight.

Fall 2008: The beginning of twenty trips to the Clinic Faraway in Minnesota.

10/08: Kennedy saw a GI doctor to get a second opinion about the hiatal hernia surgery. The doctor ordered an endoscopy, which confirmed the very large hernia. Prior to the procedure, she remembers the doctor not believing her that she had one because it hadn't shown up on the CT scan. After the endoscopy she remembers asking the people in recovery if she had a large hernia or not. The response was she absolutely did, and nobody in the room would forget it. Apparently during the procedure Kennedy threw up all over everybody in the room. That's what they get for not believing her! To test her stomach function, the doctor ordered a gastric emptying test, where they discovered and diagnosed her with gastroparesis. This is a condition where your stomach will not empty on its own. After trying Reglan, to which she had an allergic reaction, she was put on Domperidone, which allowed her to eat again … thank goodness! The only issue with this drug is it has to be ordered from out of the country.

11/08: Kennedy saw a dermatologist for her hair. They said that it would grow back and was the result of the trauma she had been through. They checked her entire body, which resulted in the removal of two suspicious foot moles. One was between her toes and the other was on the bottom of the same foot. This required many stitches. After returning home from this trip to the Clinic Faraway, the wounds from those procedures opened within twenty-four hours. Eventually they closed, but they were nasty wounds for a very long time.

2/09: Kennedy had a vestibulectomy at the Clinic Faraway for the non-healing vulvorvaginal fissure.

2/09: After coming home from the vaginal surgery at the Clinic Faraway, Kennedy was in extreme pain after being in the house for only twenty-four hours. At the recommendation of Dr. Kathryn Smith, who is a gynecologist at a university and also a friend, she made an appointment with Dr. Stephen Hopkinson. Kennedy needed a GYN closer to home. Dr. Hopkinson would turn out to be a huge blessing as he promised from the first meeting that he wouldn't ditch the Olivers, and he never did!

4/09: On one of Austin and Kennedy's last trips to the Clinic Faraway, she saw a neurologist for her constant brain zaps. These were lightning-bolt-type flashes that occurred in a very specific part of her brain. They were very painful and caused her face to feel numb. The neurologist said they were migraines with no known cause.

7/17/09: Dr. Hopkinson recommended a surgery to remove the non-healing area of vulvar granulation tissue from the vestibulectomy. He thought it would be an easy fix. After this surgery Kennedy did not heal and the wound was nasty.

7/30/09: At Dr. Hopkinson's recommendation, Kennedy had a consult with another GYN for a second opinion on the non-healing vaginal wound. He told her to wear gloves to bed and stop scratching herself! Dr. Evil with a capital EVIL!

8/26/09: Kennedy had a consult with dermatology to see if they could shed some light on the non-healing vaginal wound, which was unrevealing.

10/23/09: Kennedy's wound was not healing and very painful. Dr. Hopkinson recommended a repeat surgery to repair the non-healing area using a flap reconstruction. Dr. Hopkinson received assistance from his partner. The surgery was done on Kennedy's birthday, which they thought was going to be a good thing. However, this surgery was complicated by Kennedy receiving a gift of an extremely large vulvar hematoma! In layman's terms, that would be called an out of control interior bleed. It was the size of a small football between her legs! She couldn't wear her own underwear because it was so huge! On top of it, Kennedy also developed a quarter-size bleeding ulcer up inside the vaginal wall. Nobody really knows where that came from. Are you kidding me?

10/30/09: Because of the extreme nature of the hematoma, Kennedy was taken back to the OR to evacuate it. This left Kennedy with a very large open wound that required daily packing and unpacking. This meant Austin and Kennedy would have to make daily trips to Dr. Hopkinson's clinic— not easy when you are sitting on a huge open wound!

11/09: Because this wound was not diminishing, Dr. Hopkinson suggested that Kennedy try a wound vacuum. He had never used one of these before in this area. If you can, imagine a vacuum on your open-wounded crotch. This was extremely painful! The idea was to get the wound to heal from the inside out. It worked up to a point. They got the wound down to a smaller size, but it became impossible for it to close completely.

1/10: Kennedy had been away from her high school math teaching job for two years. She was originally only supposed to be gone for six weeks! Her school district was very supportive but told her that if she didn't get back to work by January she would lose her job. Austin had retired from his teaching position during this time to help care for Kennedy. She went back to work in January with three bleeding vaginal ulcers. Yes, two ulcers somehow turned into three! She had also lost a lot of weight and was very weak. If Kennedy didn't get back to work, the Olivers would lose their insurance and a whole lot more! Austin dropped her off every morning and picked her up every afternoon. She often went from school to the doctor, where they would attempt to stitch, cauterize the wounds, or do whatever they could to stop the bleeding. She would then return to teach the very next day. It was only by the grace of God that she made it through this time. We still don't know how she did it. She came every day, taught every hour while in extreme pain, and would often have to leave the minute the kids did to go get stitched, glued, or cauterized.

4/5/10: After being back at school for nine weeks, the school granted Kennedy another medical leave because Dr. Hopkinson recommended that she go back to the OR to reattempt a surgical closure of the non-healing areas on the vulva and vagina. This surgery again was not successful. This would be surgery #9, not including the foot surgery at the Clinic Faraway or the many failed procedures attempted in the clinic.

5/24/10: Kennedy had a consult with a physical therapist for chronic pelvic pain. She attempted physical therapy, but it seemed to make things worse.

6/25/10: By this time because of the breakdown of the surgical wound, Dr. Steve attempted to stitch the wound up at the clinic. Over the course of the previous several years, this had been attempted too many times to count.

7/15/10: For some reason, because Kennedy and Austin knew that they could not live like they were living, they kept agreeing to these surgeries. It sounds a little crazy when you put it on paper, but it felt like it was their only hope. Dr. Hopkinson made a final attempt at closure of the non-healing vulvovaginal wounds with assistance of another doctor. This was surgery #10 in two and a half years. Again, this was not successful, and the wounds opened soon after being home from surgery. Why didn't anyone question the environment in which they lived? God only knows …

Her vagina is still a mess. The Olivers never dreamed they would feel so completely comfortable using the word *vagina* in their daily conversations. The next recommendation was total vaginal reconstruction. They consulted with a doctor for this but struggled to go that route.

8/2/10: Kennedy was still not healed, and it was time to return to school. Kennedy would teach the entire 2010/2011 school year with three nasty, bleeding wounds down under. She was in constant pain! She walked very slowly, constantly holding her lower left pelvic side, and looked sick.

At the beginning of the school year, Lucy's teacher alerted the Olivers that Lucy was having a hard time staying awake in school. They took her to the doctor. She had a very significant sinus infection without any symptoms. They could not get it cleared up. Lucy and Chloë, who were in fourth and second grades at this point, both really struggled in school. Lucy would cry at night because she said she was dumb. She would read several times a week with Kennedy's mom.

Grandma felt horrible for Lucy because she had such a hard time even staying awake, much less reading.

3/11: The Olivers traveled for a consult to a Faraway Clinic in Michigan with a GYN specialist. They had made twenty-plus trips to the Clinic Faraway, had hundreds of appointments where they lived, and also drove to another state to the Faraway Clinic for another opinion. The Olivers were desperate for help! The doctors in the other state were at a loss too but thought that now the lesions in her vagina were eating through to her colon … not good. In fact, this would have been very bad!

5/11: They came back home where she had a colonoscopy to rule out a hole between her vagina and colon. There wasn't one there yet, but the doctor said that the area was a complete mess and that there was a risk of a hole down the road. These are not medical terms, but in Kennedy's own words.

6/11: Here comes the big kicker—Austin's colon ruptured out of the blue! He was instantly sick to death … literally! *This rocked their world!* Austin was Kennedy's caretaker and appeared to be very healthy prior to this. They had no previous warnings that Austin had issues; in fact, he had a colonoscopy not too long before this that was unrevealing.

6/29/11: Three days after being admitted to the hospital, Austin's temperature soared to 104 degrees, and they told Kennedy that he needed to have emergency surgery to save his life. It was one of the scariest times in their lives. They took Austin by ambulance to a bigger hospital, where the doctors performed emergency surgery and took part of his colon. He ended up with a colostomy. Austin lost twenty pounds almost instantly and was in the hospital for two weeks. People in their lives totally took over. They needed an army to keep them from falling apart!

7/2011: Austin came home from the hospital and immediately had healing issues. He could not stay awake and was extremely lethargic. On top of it, his very large wound opened and got infected.

8/11: Both Dr. Stephen Hopkinson and Dr. Thomas Kennedy, who the Olivers had seen as their chiropractor and nutrition expert through all these years of health issues, recommended that they get their house checked. They initially did a check for radon, which revealed nothing. Dr. Tom then came to their house where he discovered that something was contaminating their master bedroom. He told them to call the gas company. They did that immediately and found a very significant gas leak. It was fixed that very day.

9/11: Guess what? Everyone started healing! Kennedy's vaginal ulcers went away within a couple of months! They had been there for years! Austin woke up and began to heal. Their girls, Lucy and Chloë, who had very delayed learning issues, started to do better in school. To be clear, both girls could not read, were in the lowest math groups, and could not concentrate at all. The Olivers had hired tutors for them since they started school. Remember, this started when the girls were two and four. The gas leak was found and fixed six years later, making them eight and 1ten. Lucy's sinus issues also cleared up.

1/12: Austin had his colostomy takedown surgery to reconnect his colon.

Summer 2012: The Olivers got their lives back! It would be the first summer since 2005 that they all felt healthy! The girls had made significant progress in school, and it was the first summer that they didn't have to meet weekly with a tutor to try to help them learn. Both girls now read above grade level and they are both in the highest level of math! The gas leak totally affected their brains!

8/12: Austin had surgery to repair a hernia that developed after his second surgery. He healed normally.

The Olivers enjoyed a year without any significant health issues; however, because of what they had endured, Kennedy has permanent damage to her stomach and her vaginal function will never be the same. Those parts are forever messed up! She continues to deal with horrible stomach function and continues to take medication every time that she wants to eat anything. If she doesn't take the medication, then she gets nauseous and eventually throws up. They still must get this medication outside of the United States because it is not approved here.

Fall 2013: Unfortunately, Kennedy found out that the stomach medication, if taken over a long period of time, can cause a major production of breast fluid. She started to notice a strange sensation in her breasts and the story continues— the gas leak that keeps on giving!

11/2013: Beginning of left nipple bloody discharge.

Winter 2013: Nobody felt great, but we couldn't put our finger on it. Seriously?

Chloë: stomachaches

Lucy: mono-like symptoms
Austin: extreme fatigue
Kennedy: extreme fatigue and breast issues

2/14: Kennedy had a mammogram. The result was unable to rule out cancer. The actual mammogram experience was something out of a scary movie. When pressure was applied to the breasts, both started expressing bloody fluid. The test revealed crazy activity under the left nipple. I don't think "crazy activity" was the exact medical jargon for the test result. At any rate, because of this, the doctor recommended surgery to rule out cancer.

2/14: Kennedy had breast surgery. This was called left side nipple duct excision … lovely! The surgeon cut open the entire nipple and removed the enlarged ducts.

2/21: One week after surgery, the breast exploded—literally, it blew open and sprayed bloody fluid all over their bathroom! We're talking a crazy amount of fluid! It was something out of a horror movie! At the exact same time, Austin came down with acute stomach pain. Austin and Kennedy had to tape her breast back together and deal with Austin's issues because he was in extreme pain. The same day that the breast exploded, they made an ER visit for Austin where they determined that he had acute pancreatitis. Austin is not a drinker and never had any previous issues with his pancreas. They didn't even know that acute pancreatitis was a thing you could get! For peace of mind, they decided to call the gas company. Guess what? They detected a gas leak in their furnace that had probably been there all winter! No wonder they all felt like garbage! Are you kidding me?

Thankfully, Austin and the girls immediately started feeling better. Kennedy was another story ...

4/14: Because of Kennedy's breast blowing up, she was left with a very large open wound on her left breast that continually drained fluid. The doctor tried to close it in clinic, but the wound reopened because of the fluid pressure within twenty-four hours. The doctor recommended another left side duct excision, so back to surgery she went. Again, one week after surgery, the breast exploded. Why must we repeat horrific traumatic experiences? At this point, the doctor did not know the cause of the fluid building up and did not realize that the right breast had the same fluid buildup. They saw an endocrinologist who didn't know why this was happening and had never seen anything like it. On no! Are you kidding me?

To add insult to injury, Kennedy then came down with shingles—can anyone say nightmare? If you've never had shingles before, it's really painful! Especially, when it's in addition to breast explosions with big open wounds! Kennedy was in really rough shape. As you can imagine, this made teaching very difficult. The school district allowed her to go to half time until the end of the school year. It was pretty amazing that Kennedy could teach at all, but she again found the strength from somewhere. Does anyone know from whom she got that strength? Duh ... from God, of course. Kennedy will be the first one to tell you, "I am not a strong person on my own!"

5/14: Kennedy saw a doctor who is a general practitioner and also a lactation expert. She knew about the stomach medication causing this breast fluid condition and connected all the dots. This meant that as long as Kennedy was taking the stomach medication, she would have this breast condition. The wound on the left breast would not close because it was constantly draining fluid, and the right breast was now spraying fluid at will … crazy! Kennedy had a GI consult to see if fixing the stomach was an option. This would mean another serious surgery, where they would implant a pacemaker to force her stomach to push food through. This surgery was not guaranteed and seemed very risky. Actually, what surgery isn't? The only other alternative would be to remove her breasts.

7/18/14: The Olivers opted for a bilateral mastectomy. This would be surgery #18 in her lifetime. She lost her breasts, ultimately, because of a natural gas leak in their home.

8/14–11/15: Unfortunately, Kennedy would have to endure four more breast surgeries after the mastectomy because of circumstances out of their control—actually, isn't everything out of our control? Needless to say, it's been a long haul. That's life, people!

Summer 2016: Kennedy set a goal to write a book. From June to August, she got it written! The process for writing this book was extremely healing, very painful, but cathartic for all of Team Oliver. Lucy and Chloë, at ages thirteen and fifteen, were able to read the story and actually understand the details of what their family went through. Everyone was finally able to feel the emotions, have conversations, and process what this experience gave to them. All four have agreed that the perspective they now have is something you can't put a price on. It's an absolute blessing!

Team Oliver no longer lives in the house they built in 2005. They purchased a lot and built right across the street because they love the neighborhood so much. They sold the house just because they needed a change. This was a very healing move forward! They have become good friends with the beautiful family that bought the house that changed their lives forever and blessed them beyond measure! The present owners have two adorable little girls themselves, and in case you are wondering, they have had no gas leaks and no problems, thank goodness! Austin remains retired, Kennedy is now in her twenty-sixth year of teaching high school mathematics, Lucy is now a junior in high school and was recently inducted into the National Honor Society, and Chloë continues to get straight A's and is a freshman in high school. Oh, and Cooper is still the best dog ever! They all feel absolutely blessed with sometimes an "Are you kidding me?" mixed in.

Life is hard, people, but God is oh so good!

Where will life take them next?

God only knows …

CPSIA information can be obtained
at www.ICGtesting.com
Printed in the USA
FSHW04n1835220418
47270FS